About the Book

On a rainy Friday afternoon in May, 1889, Megan Maxwell sat on the window seat in the attic of her large house, watching the water level rise in the street below. The spoiled daughter of a prominent family in Johnstown, Pennsylvania, Megan was more preoccupied with thoughts of her first grown-up party the night before than by the unusual amount of water swirling by. She little realized that at that very moment the South Fork Dam had broken, unleashing the tremendous mass of water that caused the great Johnstown Flood.

In an exciting narrative based on eyewitness accounts, *The Terrible Wave* chronicles Megan's experiences from the moment the incredible wall of water hit her home, carrying her off on a sodden mattress. Separated from her family, Megan found refuge on a raft with a collection of people she would never have otherwise met: Brian, who was saving his earnings as a delivery boy to go to college; Septimus Shaw, an elderly watchmaker; and Tom and Daisy, two actors from a road company. As the hours passed and Megan and her companions were gradually able to begin searching for their family and friends, Megan came to realize that they all needed one another and that she too must share responsibility with her companions.

Illustrations by Charles Robinson dramatize this highly readable and accurate account of the famed disaster and one girl's reactions to it.

The Terrible Wave

BY

MARDEN DAHLSTEDT

ILLUSTRATED BY CHARLES ROBINSON

COWARD, McCANN & GEOGHEGAN, INC.
NEW YORK

for Dick and Ellen

The great flood of Johnstown, Pennsylvania,
has been considered by many to have been
one of the world's greatest disasters.
Though the characters in this book are
fictional, the major incidents depicted
are true.
The South Fork Dam broke at 3:10 P.M. on
Friday, May 31, 1889. It took nearly an
hour for the terrible wave to reach
Johnstown and less than half an hour
for the entire city to be destroyed.
This book begins at the moment the South
Fork Dam broke.

1

3:10 P.M., Friday, May 31, 1889

"If it doesn't soon stop raining," Megan said firmly, "I am just going to spit!"

She was kneeling on the window seat, her face pressed against the streaming glass of the attic window.

"Megan Maxwell!" Aunt Ella's voice was sharp. "You watch your language."

"Come on, Megs . . . let's see you spit."

Her small brother, Timothy, was genuinely interested.

Aunt Ella wheeled about from the cupboard where she was stacking linen.

"And you, young man," she scolded, "you have no call to be repeating bad language."

"What's wrong with spitting, Aunt Ella?"

His round eyes were innocent.

"It's not nice, that's what's wrong with it. And your sister ought to know better. Megan, you apologize this minute."

Megan hadn't even turned around. Through the lashing rain, her eye caught the sight of several people running in the street below. From up so high, and screened by the fast-falling drops, they looked like little tin wind-up dolls. Water covered the street almost to the curbstone.

"Megan, did you hear me?"

"Yes, Aunt Ella . . . I'm sorry," she mumbled.

Aunt Ella was such an everlasting prissy bore! She wished her mother would come home from visiting relatives, and then Aunt Ella could leave. Being cooped in because of the rain didn't help either.

"I think there's going to be a flood," she announced glumly, turning away from the window.

"Johnstown floods every time there's a rain," remarked Aunt Ella. "I keep telling your father he ought to move up to Altoona."

Megan paid no attention to this. She slid to the floor like a sulky child, her back against the window seat, and folded her arms.

"Kit and I were going downtown to the store," she said to no one in particular, "and now this dumb rain."

"Well, I hope your father gets the merchandise moved up high in case the water does come up," Aunt Ella said.

Megan's father owned Johnstown's largest and finest department store. All of the Maxwell children loved to go there, for his clerks smiled and scurried to please them, and they always came home with some special trinket or treasure.

Leaning her head back against the worn plush cushion, Megan closed her eyes and let her mind return, for the hundredth time, to last night's party. Yesterday had been a memorable day altogether. There had been the Memorial Day parade in the morning, and decorating the graves, and then Kit's party in the evening.

It was her first real almost-grown-up party. Thinking back on it now, it had been part great fun and part pure misery. Why is it, she wondered, that things are so often like that?

Her best friend, Kit Huber, had been celebrating her fifteenth birthday, and Mrs. Huber had allowed Megan to help Kit plan the affair. The girls had worked for a month making favors. They had spent hours stringing garlands of paper flowers to decorate the Hubers' two large parlors and had driven their cook nearly to distraction with last-minute changes of menu.

Megan's dress had been the prettiest at the party. Her mother's dressmaker had really outdone herself: Four organ-pipe pleats fell to a tiny train at the back, and the primrose silk leg o'mutton sleeves and the high collar were trimmed with heavy lace. She had been allowed to wear her long dark hair piled high, with a fresh camellia entwined in primrose satin ribbon.

It was a major social event of the season, and all of the best families in Johnstown were there. Kit's brother John was home from Princeton University with a friend. Will Alford was the handsomest boy Megan had ever seen, tall and pale, with a languid elegance of manner that made the Johnstown boys seem dull and awkward. He'd danced with her only once, though, and spent most of the evening standing by the great crystal punch bowl talking with John.

Megan's face burned at the memory. She remembered talking too loud as she waltzed past him with another partner and flirting outrageously with Charley Fitch to capture Will's attention. It seemed to her last night that she was the belle of the ball, but now, thinking about it, she felt silly and ashamed.

She remembered saying loudly to Kit as she left, "Let's go to Papa's store tomorrow. He's got some marvelous new lace." She was hoping Will Alford would hear and know that her father was the richest man in Johnstown. Maybe then he'll realize I'm not just a nobody, she had thought.

"Hey, Megs, look at this," Timothy called, breaking into her sorry thoughts. "I made a parade!"

Megan looked across the enormous attic room. Fully half

of it was a magnificent playhouse. It had been built first for Megan, and now that she was fifteen and too old for it, it was used by her sisters, Grace and Louisa and little Fanny. The furnishings had come from the store—little tables and chairs and beds, a miniature piano that really played, and a complete kitchen, with tiny china dishes, copper pans, and a black iron stove.

Megan threaded her way across the tiny rooms to Timothy's corner.

"Look," he said, "it's just like the parade yesterday."

She perched on the back of Timothy's great wooden rocking horse with its red velvet saddle. On the floor he had lined up a row of toys in imitation of the Memorial Day parade.

"This one's supposed to be Papa." He pointed to a single lead soldier in a scarlet coat out in front of the ranks.

His father had walked in yesterday's parade with other prominent men of the town.

"Did you like the parade?" Megan asked, dropping to her knees beside him.

He was only five, and it was the first time he had been taken.

"I was sort of scared of the horses," he confided, glancing back over his shoulder at Aunt Ella and lowering his voice. "Aunt Ella pushed me way out in front so's I could see, and I was thinkin' they might kick me."

"I know," Megan said. "That always used to scare me, too, when I was little."

"An' I got splashed with mud all over," he chuckled. This memory pleased him.

The rain had stopped long enough yesterday for the parade to wind its way across town to the cemetery.

"I'll bet those flowers we put on the graves are a real mess by now," Megan said. "Seems a shame."

She bent down.

"You don't have a *train* in a parade," she said, picking up the iron toy.

Timothy snatched it from her.

"You can too, if you want. . . ." He put it back in place.

Megan rocked back on her heels.

"Oh, I am so bored!" she exclaimed.

She made her way back to the little pointed window in the gable and rubbed steam from the glass with the back of her hand.

"Tim!" she called sharply. "Come here a minute!"

When he stood beside her she lifted him up and held him close to the window.

"Look down there," she said. "The water has come up into the yard."

He strained to see through the driving rain, pressing his small round nose flat against the glass.

"Oooh, Megs," he cried. "Can I go down and wade?"

"Indeed, you cannot," Aunt Ella said.

She had crossed the room and was peering over Megan's shoulder.

"The very idea! Wanting to splash about in that filthy water. Looks like the whole Conemaugh River is out there in the street!"

She took Timothy from Megan's arms and set him on the floor.

"Now you go back and amuse yourself until your papa gets home."

With her handkerchief she rubbed the window.

"Land's sakes—getting the glass all dirty like that!"

Megan gave her one exasperated look and started toward the stairway down from the attic.

"I'll go check on Louisa and Fanny," she called back over her shoulder.

Secretly, she could hardly wait to get down to the porch to see how high the water had come. It was exciting, and she didn't want to miss anything.

As a sop to her conscience, she did stop on the second floor. Her two younger sisters were in bed with measles. Their fevers were down, the spots nearly gone, and they were cross at being made to stay in bed in a darkened room. But Papa feared that too much light would damage their eyes.

Megan opened the door softly. Through the dimness she could see two heads close together on the big bolster pillow. Exhausted by boredom, Louisa and Fanny had fallen asleep.

Closing the door gently so as not to disturb them, Megan made her way down the broad carved staircase to the first floor. Faintly, from behind the closed door to the kitchen corridor, she could hear the voice of Hulda, their house-maid, raised in song.

"A mighty forr-t-ress iss our Gott.

A bull-vark neffer fay-yel-ling. . . ."

In a thick German accent, Hulda bellowed hymn tunes all day long as she worked.

Megan snatched a shawl from the mahogany rack in the hallway and quietly opened the great double door with its long panels of etched glass. A chill wind caught the edges of the shawl. For the last day of May it was surprisingly cold.

Going over to the porch railing, she looked down. Indeed, it seemed as if Aunt Ella were right—the whole Little Conemaugh River seemed to be running down their street!

Megan heard a loud splashing. A block away she could see the ice wagon. Buttercup, the old horse that pulled it, was struggling through water almost up to her belly, and the red and gilt wagon carried six people, all strangers to

her. They were throwing off big cakes of ice to lighten the load, and the crystal blocks went floating out ahead of the wagon. How curious, Megan thought.

She waved to the people as they passed by the house. They were shouting and seemed to be in a holiday mood, waving their arms at her, but she couldn't hear what they said, for the wind carried their voices in the other direction.

This was even more exciting than the Memorial Day parade yesterday!

Megan crossed to the other side of the wide porch and peered around the corner. Their own stable stood at the rear of the house at the end of a long lawn. Here her father's fine matched pair of carriage horses lived, along with six ducks that were family pets, the innumerable families of kittens that came and went, and Senator, their big black Labrador retriever.

Both the stable and the house were like islands now. The water wasn't as deep as in the street, for they sat on higher ground, but it swirled gently everywhere. The ducks were delighted. They were paddling happily and quacking as they floated over the flower beds.

Through the open door of the stable Megan could see the shining black rumps of the horses which stood patiently in the shallow water. Senator had jumped to the top of a feed-box, the chain on his collar stretched taut. He liked to swim, but not at the end of a chain.

Maybe I'd better untie him, thought Megan, and bring the cats into the house, too. Hulda'll have a fit, but I can't help that.

She hitched up the folds of her long skirt and bunched it around her waist. Rolling up her long lace-trimmed drawers, she took off her shoes and stockings and took a first tentative step into the water.

It was muddy-looking and kind of cold, but once she was in it wasn't too bad. The water came halfway up her legs.

She splashed across the lawn, the sodden grass feeling soft and squashy beneath her bare feet.

I hope Aunt Ella doesn't see me, she thought, or I'll really catch it!

When Senator saw her coming, he started a wild barking. "Hush up," she called to him. "You'll get us both in trouble."

As she loosed his chain, the big dog licked her with great enthusiasm.

"Oh, for heaven's sake, Senator," she laughed, "as if I'm not wet enough already!"

He leaped into the water and ran in joyful circles.

Megan couldn't find the cats at first, but then she saw that they had crawled high up into the hayloft.

"Well, you'll be all right up there," she told them and started back for the porch.

It wasn't raining so hard now, so Megan took a detour through the grape arbor. It was fun wading like this—and I'm going to get scolded anyway, she told herself.

The ducks circled her, dashingly white in the brown water.

Megan finally reached the porch and discovered that the first step was under water.

Golly, she thought, it's never come this high before.

Johnstown, in the western end of Pennsylvania, lay in a triangle of land where the Stony Creek met with the Little Conemaugh to form the Conemaugh River. Great mountains thrust up all around the town in its little pocket of land, and hard rains always brought flooding to the lower parts of town. But the great Maxwell house stood on higher ground, and there had never been water here before.

Megan was reluctant to put her shoes back on, and so she sat on the edge of the porch dangling her bare legs in the water. A bed of pansies by the front walk had been nearly covered, and the little purple-and-yellow flower faces drifted upturned, swaying gently in the eddy of the current.

Just then the figure of a man in high boots came hurrying around the corner of the block. He was carrying a large black umbrella.

Oh, oh, thought Megan. It's Papa! And now I'm in for it!

2

4:00 P.M., Friday, May 31, 1889

Her father came splashing up the front walk at a half run. He was normally a sedate and dignified man, always carefully dressed, and he looked so odd, his hair plastered down by the rain, his dark suit stained with muddy water.

When Megan saw him coming she stood up quickly. There was no time to put on her shoes and stockings, but she did drop the folds of her skirt. She stood there waiting for her scolding.

"Megan! What in the world are you doing?" her father asked, shaking the raindrops from his umbrella and leaning it beside the door.

But before she could answer, he went on, "Well, never mind now. . . ."

Megan stared at him in astonishment.

A worry line creased his forehead.

"Where is everyone?" he asked.

"Well," she began, "Aunt Ella and Tim are up in the attic, and Louisa and Fanny are sleeping, and Hulda—"

Her father strode across the porch quickly and grasped her shoulders in a firm grip. "Now listen to me carefully. You must do exactly as I say, and do it quickly."

"What is it, Papa?" She was searching his face anxiously.

"I'm not sure," he said, "but I've heard that the dam has broken."

All the color drained from Megan's face. This fear had hung over their heads as long as she could remember.

Her father gripped her more tightly and attempted a smile.

"Probably it's not true—only a rumor, like all the other times. But I don't want to take the chance. I'm taking all of you up the hill, just in case. . . ."

"All right, Papa. What do you want me to do?"

"That's my girl!" He bent swiftly and kissed her cheek. "We mustn't frighten the others," he told her, "but we've got to hurry."

He started toward the front door.

"I will get Louisa and Fanny," he said, "and you run up to the attic and tell Aunt Ella to bring Timothy. But," he warned her, "don't say anything about the dam."

Megan stooped to pick up her shoes and stockings. "I'll be just a minute," she said.

Her father glanced back over his shoulder. The water had reached the third step of the porch.

"Don't bother about that," he called. "Hurry!"

There was an urgency in his voice that Megan had never heard before. It sent a tiny warning bell ringing in her mind. A small chill of fear ran down her spine.

She scooped up her shoes and stockings and followed him through the wide front hallway. Her father, who was always so dignified, was running up the stairs two at a time!

Megan raced after him. He went pounding down the up-stairs hallway to the little girls' room, and Megan continued on up to the attic. Her heart was beating fast and she was out of breath when she reached the playroom.

"Aunt Ella . . . Tim," she called. "Papa says we're all to go up to the hill right away—there's a chance—"

She was about to say "the dam has broken," but she quickly remembered her father's warning.

"The water's getting higher," she finished lamely.

Aunt Ella went on calmly arranging linens in the big walnut cupboard.

"The water won't come up to the house," she said matter-of-factly. "It never has before."

Megan had run across the room and gripped Timothy's hand.

He stared at her bare feet in astonishment.

"Megs," he wailed, stamping his foot, "you went wading and didn't take me!"

Aunt Ella spun around and was looking at Megan with a mixture of horror and disapproval.

"Megan"—she advanced toward her, a finger wagging in righteous anger—"you didn't! You didn't put your feet in that dirty water?"

Before she could answer, Megan heard her father's voice calling up the attic stairway.

"Megan, did you tell them? Hurry!"

Megan began dragging a protesting Timothy across the playroom.

"Hurry, Aunt Ella—oh, please hurry! Papa said to—"

Aunt Ella went to the stairwell and peered down.

"Edward," she shouted, "what is all this nonsense? Did you know that your daughter has been very rude and disobedient, and—"

"Blast it, Ella. Come down here!"

Even through her confusion, Megan was startled to hear the rough tone in her father's voice. He had never spoken like this before. A look of shock and hurt spread across Aunt Ella's prim face.

The three of them made their way down the attic stairs. Behind her Megan could hear the rustle of her aunt's stiff taffeta petticoats.

Her father stood in the hallway. Little Fanny, bundled into a quilt, was curled in his arms, and he held Louisa by the hand. He had thrown a blanket over her shoulders, and she was rubbing her eyes, still dazed with sleep.

"I'm sorry, Ella," Papa was saying, "but the water is getting dangerously high. I want you to bring the children and follow me. We're all going up to Green Hill."

Even Aunt Ella seemed to sense the emergency at last.

"All right, Edward," she agreed. "But I want to get my garnets, and Mother's diamond eardrops. . . ."

"There's not time," Papa said tersely. "Come . . . *now!*"

It was a strange procession that trooped down the broad staircase—a damp and water-stained papa with the two little girls in their long white ruffled nightdresses, Aunt Ella in her lace cap with its long black ribbons, Timothy dragging his toy train, and a barefoot Megan, still clutching her shoes and stockings.

"On-vard Chrisstian so-ol-jers . . ."

"Hulda!" Megan gasped. "I forgot to tell Hulda. . . ."

She thrust Timothy's hand into Aunt Ella's and ran toward the kitchen.

The great room, with its shining black stove, was warm and bright. Hulda, enveloped in a vast white apron, her wheat-colored hair screwed to a knot on the top of her head, was vigorously chopping cabbage in a big wooden bowl.

"Marr-sh-ing as to var,

"Mit de cross of Jesus . . ."

"Hulda," Megan cried, "Papa says to come right away— we're all going up to Green Hill. . . ."

A slow astonishment spread over Hulda's broad, ruddy face.

"Vat's de matter, Miss Megan? You took sick or someting?"

"Oh, Hulda! The water's coming up fast. Please come. . . ."

"But vat aboot my dinner?" Hulda gestured wildly at the kettles bubbling on the stove.

"Never mind about that," Megan said impatiently, fighting back the fear that had been uncoiling rapidly within her. She grasped Hulda's large red hand and began pulling her toward the door.

"Please, Hulda—hurry!"

Half pulling her, and assuring her that Papa wouldn't be angry, Megan finally managed to get the reluctant woman through the front hall and onto the porch.

Her father's sense of urgency had been well communicated, but now Megan felt her first real fright. Water sloshed gently over the porch floor and had begun to seep into the house. She would never have believed it could rise so fast!

She could see her father halfway down the block, holding Fanny high on his shoulder and half carrying, half dragging Louisa. Ugly brown water swirled around him waist deep, and she could hear him calling, "Come on now, follow me. . . . It's only another block to the hill. . . ."

Aunt Ella stood frozen on the front porch, still holding Timothy by the hand. The once-immaculate ruffle on her black silk dress floated about her feet like a dark fan.

"I can't," she was saying. "I won't . . . I won't . . . I simply won't go into that filthy water."

Beyond her, in the street, Megan could see a number of people splashing wildly on their way to the hill. Some of them were carrying children perched high on their shoulders. One man had a huge straw suitcase balanced on top of his derby hat, holding it with one hand while he paddled with the other. A woman who was screaming held up a silver fan with peacock eyes that whipped out in the rising wind.

For one blinding moment Megan thought of the picture in the great plush-bound Bible that stood on the parlor table —the awful picture of the Biblical Flood.

Aunt Ella turned around and ran back into the house, still hanging onto Timothy's hand. The little boy was crying.

"Come with me, all of you," she cried. "We're going back up to the attic. We'll be safe there."

"But, Aunt Ella," Megan cried frantically, "Papa said—"

"Never mind now what your papa said. We'll be much safer here than out in that water."

And so saying, Aunt Ella marched rapidly back up the stairs.

Megan was torn with conflict. Everything in her said go, do as Papa ordered. But she couldn't leave the others alone in the house.

"Oh, all right," she said desperately and turned to Hulda. "Come on, then, we'll go up to the attic."

Hulda was so bewildered by the swift succession of events and by the unprecedented sight of water in the front hallway, that she did not resist. Together they hurried up to the attic.

For some strange reason, Aunt Ella had climbed into the great walnut cupboard. She crouched there on the floor of it, holding the weeping Timothy in her arms, her face hidden against his curly head.

Megan ran quickly to the window to see if she could get a glimpse of her father.

Dimly through the rain she could see down to the end of the block where Green Hill jutted up steeply. A number of people were clambering up its sides, clutching at small shrubs and tree roots to help pull themselves up the mud-slick slope.

She saw a man holding two white blurs, which she thought could be Fanny and Louisa, and frightened, she could see her father attempting to push his way through the swirling water back toward the house. She flung open the window.

"No, Papa," she called frantically through the strange rumbling sound she heard. "No . . . no . . . go back . . . we're all right. . . ."

From somewhere now she could hear a shrill, insistent whistle that never stopped.

She started to gesture to him to go back, when suddenly she saw her father stop. The water was nearly to his armpits. He held up both his hands in the air for a second. Then, turning, he began to flounder through the water back toward the hill.

Megan wasn't sure that he had even seen her.

She turned to glance in the direction of her father had been looking.

It was at that moment she saw the terrible wave coming.

3

Megan was, in fact, one of the few people in Johnstown that day who actually *saw* the gigantic wave that destroyed the entire city.

At first all she could see was a sinister black mist. It rolled toward the house like billowing smoke. For a moment Megan thought there must be a huge fire somewhere.

But the noise convinced her it was something else—a deep, heavy rumbling, mixed with a grinding sound, like some enormous mill wheel churning.

The black fog curled swiftly over the house, and then the air seemed to clear for one split second. There, almost on top of her, was a huge wall of debris-filled water, much higher than the house!

Megan spun around, the cry dying in her throat.

The doors of the tall walnut linen press were still open, and hunched on the floor, Aunt Ella was shielding Timothy with her own body. Megan could hear her aunt's voice, high and thin, praying ardently. "Oh, dear merciful Lord, save us . . . save us. . . ."

Hulda, numb with terror, knelt by Timothy's rocking horse, her hands folded over the velvet saddle. She was praying in German. Megan could hear her voice through the ominous rumble, over and over. *"Mein gross Gott . . . mein gross Gott. . . ."*

She could see the tiny toy copper pans on the playhouse wall begin to shiver. A soft film of plaster dust began to fall from the ceiling as gently as snow.

Suddenly there was a tremendous crash. It sounded as if the whole house had been caught in a vast grinding machine. Megan saw the boards of the attic floor split open. A surge of oily yellow water gushed up, foaming at the edges like old lace.

Then it seemed as if the air were filled with flying objects. Trunks whirled by, wicked-looking boards splintered with nails, showers of broken glass winged a thousand tiny arrows, linens flapped like eerie white birds, chairs with the legs torn off went whistling by. Everything in the attic seemed to be whirling through the air.

Megan ducked her head and shielded her body with her arms against the careening debris. The floor beneath her feet heaved mightily and then suddenly dropped.

Wildly, Megan reached up, her hands grasping for anything to cling to. She found herself swinging from a rough board, the lower half of her body submerged in water.

How long she clung there in the heaving darkness she would never know. She was choking and spitting as the evil water surged about her, splashing over her face.

After what seemed a lifetime in the thunderous blackness, Megan lifted her head. Far above her she could see a glimmer of dirty gray light.

She wasn't even thinking now. Painfully she began to crawl toward the light with a kind of blind animal instinct. Clinging with one hand, she would reach out with the other until she found some new thing to grasp. And so inch by inch she worked her way through the tangle of shattered wood toward the tiny wedge of light above her. The crack of snapping boards and the terrible thunderous roar still filled her ears.

The wedge of light suddenly widened. There was a long hiss and gurgle of rushing water. Megan felt herself being pushed, as if by a mighty hand, through the jagged crack between darkness and light. The force of the movement sent her flying. Flailing her arms, she rushed through the rainy air.

This was the worst thing of all, this feeling of total helplessness. Even the jagged boards to cling to had been comforting compared to this. With a sickening thud, she landed, sprawling on something horribly soft and squashy.

Too frightened to move, she simply lay there, her eyes closed, her breath coming in great choking sobs. Her mind had completely ceased to function. Drawing her knees up under her chin, she circled them with her arms. She curled herself up small, whimpering like an animal in pain.

Finally, bit by bit, her brain began to register again. The first thing she became aware of was the cold. It was incredible, biting deep down into the very marrow of her bones. She hugged herself tighter to fight it. Slowly she realized that her clothes were soaking wet. Rain beat down heavily and without mercy upon her, flattening her long hair against her shoulders.

Last of all she noticed the smell. It was so horrible, a sour and rotten stench, that instinctively she raised her head in recoil from it. With her head up, she finally opened her eyes.

She was crouched on a sodden, mud-stained mattress!

The mattress itself seemed to be buoyed up on a tangle of broken boards and tree branches, making a kind of crazy, lopsided raft. It was floating on a sea of fearfully churning dark water that seemed to stretch out in all directions.

Before she could get her bearings, something heavy crashed into the side of the precariously balanced mattress. It tilted with a sickening lurch. Megan grabbed frantically for the edge, her fingers digging deep into the spongy cotton. Whatever struck went lurching away on the current, and the "raft" righted itself.

Gasping, Megan saw that it had been the great dark bulk of a horse, slack and floating on its side, its large, soft eyes staring sightlessly into the rain. The trunk of a giant tree came rushing past, its roots waving above the water like a hundred searching fingers. It snagged the horse's body, and together they spun off down the rushing current, the horse bobbing up and down like a grotesque toy. Megan stared after it in fascinated horror.

The makeshift raft miraculously continued to float. Megan discovered that if she was careful she could get on her hands and knees without tilting it too much. This made it easier to see, and although darkness seemed to be falling fast, Megan began to search in vain for some familiar object.

She had no idea where she was. For a moment she believed that she had died and was in some peculiar sort of cold, wet hell. And then she decided that the world must have come to an end, that Judgment Day was at hand, and that she was the last person left alive on earth. These thoughts raced each other through her stunned mind as she crouched on her knees, clutching the swaying mattress, too frightened even to cry out.

The din around her was tremendous. It was an entirely unhuman sound—cracking, grinding, roaring, together with

the dreadful sucking, sloshing noise of the dark water which surrounded her.

And then Megan heard a human voice!

The bulk of a floating building loomed up to one side of her out of the driving rain. She could see a small group of people leaning out of an opening in it. They were waving their arms and shouting.

"Over here . . . over here. . . ."

A man was struggling with something. She could see dimly that he was trying to pull loose a long board from somewhere behind him. Finally he managed to work it out, and holding one end, he thrust the other toward her across the gulf of swirling water.

"Grab onto this," he shouted.

Holding the mattress with one hand, Megan reached out with the other.

"Grab it, and hang on for dear life," he yelled. "We'll pull you in. . . ."

The end of the board was about a yard's length away from her. Cautiously Megan edged nearer to the rim of the tilting mattress. The board was about a foot away now.

And then, quite suddenly, a fierce eddy of water caught her small raft, swung it around, and sent it spinning off in the opposite direction.

"Oh, my God. . . ."

She heard the high, thin wail from someone in the group. Her rescuers seemed to vanish in the rainy mist.

After a few moments the motion ceased. Megan once again dared to raise her head and look about. The eddy had carried her to a quiet stretch of water, and the mattress was floating peacefully, as if on a pond. The awful lurching had stopped.

A piano drifted beside her, its white keys looking like a great grinning mouth. Megan stared at it uncomprehendingly. It was a nightmare world. Nothing seemed real anymore.

And then Megan saw a sight that would stay with her for the rest of her life. Later, out of that whole hideous, confused time, she would remember this most vividly.

About twenty yards from where she floated on quiet water, there seemed to be a rapidly flowing current. Barrels and boards, rooftops, fences, trunks—all sorts of unimaginable debris were rushing swiftly past her.

Suddenly a large platform appeared. It might have been the floor of a house. In the center of it was an open Saratoga trunk, and kneeling about the trunk in a circle, busily packing it with articles of food and clothing, were a man and a woman, a boy and a girl.

Megan recognized them. It was Mr. Mussante, the fruit vendor from whom her mother always bought fresh produce. He came to their street each Friday morning, his handcart piled high with golden lemons, clusters of rich purple grapes, crinkle-skinned melons, mounds of apples. She knew his wife, too, Mama Mussante, who knelt beside him now, and Vito and Angela, his merry-eyed children. She had often seen them when she went with her mother to the small, sweet-smelling little store with strings of red onions hanging from the ceiling and vegetables in wooden bins.

"Oh, Mr. Mussante," Megan called at the top of her lungs, "help me ... please ... it's me, Megan Maxwell. ..."

She watched, incredulous, as the floor was carried past her. The Mussante family never raised their eyes from their task but continued steadily to pack their trunk. They sailed out of sight, still busily engaged.

Megan had been aware for the past several minutes that

the mattress beneath her was becoming dangerously soggy. It was so heavy with water that only the tangle of branches and boards underneath was keeping it afloat.

I've got to get off this thing soon, Megan thought desperately.

Feeling was beginning to return to her numbed mind and with it the realization of her precarious position. And now came a fierce will to survive.

Just then a small white house hove into view. A man was sitting astride the peaked rooftop, his long legs dangling on either side of the slope. He was clinging to the remnant of a brick chimney that reared up in the middle.

The rooftop looked at that moment large and safe and comfortable.

"Oh, help me . . . help me . . ." called Megan once again.

In desperation she lay on her stomach, and with her hands she tried to paddle the mattress toward the rooftop.

The man looked at her, a long, sad, searching glance, and just shook his head. The house drifted past her.

"Oh, you terrible, awful man," shouted Megan. "I hate you . . . I hate you. . . ."

She dropped her face against the sodden mattress and wept harsh and bitter tears.

4

Megan's whole body shook with the violence of her sobs. She was thoroughly frightened, not only by the danger she knew herself to be in, but even more by a deep and dreadful loneliness. For the first time in her entire life she was completely and unutterably alone. She had no idea where Timothy and Aunt Ella might be. She had last seen them crouched in the big linen press. Had her father reached Green Hill? Was Green Hill under water, too? And Hulda, kneeling beside the rocking horse—where was Hulda?

Slowly she became aware that her body was not being shaken by sobs alone. The mattress was heaving under her. Once again she raised her head and looked about.

Her frantic paddling to bring herself nearer to the man on the rooftop had shifted the raft out of the quiet backwater. Now she was moving again in the rapid current of the mainstream of water.

The debris under the mattress shifted and lurched to one side, tilting steeply. Gasping, Megan clutched for the high side and crawled slowly across the spongy mass.

To her astonishment she found herself looking directly into a human face!

The current had carried her close to a long wooden building that was floating along like an ark. From the narrow windows in its side Megan could see at least twenty people staring at her. She stared back, mute, too defeated to even cry out.

The face she had looked into belonged to a young man.

As if she were watching a play on the stage, she saw him turn to some men who stood behind him. He pointed toward Megan. The men shook their heads. They seemed to be arguing about something. Megan could not hear what they were saying, for the distance between the building and her mattress was growing wider.

Then she saw the young man climb onto the windowsill. One of the older men clutched at his arm. They struggled for a second. Blown on the wind, in tattered fragments of sound, Megan could hear their shouting.

"You'll never make it, boy. . . ."

". . . let 'er go. . . ."

"Come back, you damn fool. . . ."

For one long second the young man stood poised on the window ledge. Then Megan saw his body arc, drop, and disappear into the yellow water.

In her numb terror, she was puzzled by the whole scene. Before she had time to sort out properly what was happening, Megan felt an enormous lurch at one side of her mattress raft. She gave a sharp cry and turned around.

A wet, dark head appeared, sleek as a seal, and then the rest of a soaking and sizable body followed. Working his way on his stomach like a snake, he inched his way to the center of the mattress. It was the young man from the building!

"By golly," he panted, "it's not much of a craft you've got here."

Megan stared at him astounded, unable to speak.

He peered at her through a tangle of wet hair.

"Can you swim?" he demanded.

Still dumb, Megan shook her head.

He had crawled to a sitting position now, and shaking the water from his eyes like a huge dog, he peered about. Their distance from the wooden building was widening rapidly. Its windows were still crowded with heads, and a faint cheer went up.

"Toss a line," yelled the young man.

A few of the heads vanished from the windows and after a long moment reappeared. A coil of rope curled through the air. It fell short, and one of the men dragged it back through the water for a second try.

But at that moment came a horrifying grinding crash!

The mattress began to spin madly, like a Fourth of July Catherine wheel. The young man grabbed Megan and threw himself on top of her, protecting her with his body. They went reeling off in a sickening rush of water.

When their wild careening finally stopped, the young man raised his head. Megan dared to open her eyes.

Where the wooden building had been was only a crazy pile of jagged timbers. A railway coach lay jammed against it. There was no sign of any people.

The young man gripped Megan firmly by the arm and pulled her around to face him.

"Don't look," he commanded in a shaky voice.

Megan lowered her eyes. She made no sound but began to shake uncontrollably. He shook her roughly.

"Now, you just stop that . . . hear!"

"I . . . c-c-can't," she stuttered.

"Yes, you can," he said firmly. He took her face in his hands and brushed back her long dark hair.

"And since it looks as if we're going to be riding this thing

together for a while, you'd better tell me who you are. I'm
Brian O'Meara."

With great effort, Megan tried to control her shivering
and the quaver in her voice.

"H-h-how do you d-d-do," she stammered. "I'm . . . I'm
Megan Maxwell."

"Well, now, I'm pleased to make your acquaintance," said
Brian with an odd formality.

As he spoke Megan lifted her eyes and really looked at
him for the first time. Close up, he was younger than she
had thought. He was tall and sturdy, with a wide-open fresh-
colored face and sparkling deep-blue eyes. Now his thick
black hair was plastered down, and his clothing was torn
and sodden. C795909 co. schools
She was about to speak again, when suddenly he pointed.
"Look," he cried.

A short distance away and bearing down on them rapidly
was a large farm wagon. It looked like one of those big flats
on wheels used by farmers to bring in the hay harvest. It
was floating along nicely like a large solid raft, and
crouched in the center of it were two women and an old
man.

Brian reached for Megan's hand.

"Look, now," he said quickly, "you grab hold of me
around the waist and hang on. We're going to get on that
wagon."

He edged nearer the side of the mattress, motioning to
Megan to follow. The whole mass began to tilt dangerously.
The wagon was nearly beside them now. The old man had
seen them and seemed to sense what they were trying to do.
He crawled to the edge of the wagon and stretched out his
arm.

"Catch hold of me, lad," he called.

Now they were side by side, almost touching.

"Hang on," Brian cried to Megan.

With a great heave he pushed against the mattress and flung himself headlong onto the wagon, dragging Megan like a pack on his back.

The force of their leap had knocked the old man flat, and for a moment the three of them lay in a tangled, sodden heap. Finally, panting, they crawled up to a sitting position. Brian grinned at Megan.

"Lord, girl," he gasped, "you're a sight heavier than you look!"

Megan managed a weak smile.

It felt so good to have something solid under her. The wagon bed was wet but firm and comforting.

The old man was looking at both of them.

"Yes . . . well . . . it's rather a good thing we happened by."

Megan and Brian looked where he was pointing. The pile of debris beneath their mattress had broken up, and they saw the whole thing dissolve slowly and sink into the darkening water without a sound.

The old man began to crawl toward the center of the wagon.

"Come away from the edge," he cautioned. "There will be less chance of it tilting."

Megan and Brian slid carefully across the splintery planks to where the old man had joined the two women. One, middle-aged and plump, with a frizz of gray hair, was sitting upright, rocking back and forth and moaning. She paid no attention to them. The other lay on her back, her eyes closed, her face white and slack. She was young and pretty. A man's heavy tweed coat had been wrapped around her.

Megan looked at the old man in awe.

"Is she . . . is she . . . dead?" she whispered.

He shook his head solemnly.

"No," he replied. "She fainted. She's broken her leg, I think. Poor dear, from the pain of it. . . ."

His voice trailed off. He looked at Brian with a mute appeal.

"I'm glad you're here, lad," he said simply.

Brian stared at the unconscious girl for a moment. Then he stretched out his hand.

"Brian O'Meara, sir. And this is Megan Maxwell."

The old man and the young one shook hands formally.

"My name is Septimus Shaw. And may I present Mrs. Alderson"—he nodded to the middle-aged woman, who still paid them not the slightest heed—"and this poor girl—well, I don't know her. . . ."

It was only much later, when she thought about it all, that Megan was filled with wonder at this curious little scene of grave introductions carried on at the height of one of the world's greatest disasters! At the time it seemed the natural thing to do.

The wagon continued to float rather slowly now. Occasionally something would bump against it, but it was heavy and steady enough to withstand the blows. The rain had slackened somewhat to a thin, chill drizzle, and darkness was advancing rapidly.

In every direction was incredible desolation. For the first time since the terrible wave had struck—it seemed centuries ago to her—Megan really looked about her. The whole of Johnstown was a giant mass of rubble floating in an enormous lake of churning, greasy water. It seemed impossible that a whole town could be so utterly destroyed.

"Mr. Shaw, sir, do you have any idea where we are?"

Brian's voice seemed to come from somewhere miles away through the numbing fog that filled Megan's mind.

Septimus Shaw nodded. "I have figured—it seems to me

at any rate—that we must be somewhere near the Kernville section," he replied. "I have been looking for some landmark and"—he pointed back in the direction from which they had come—"over there, see, it looks like the steeple of the Methodist church."

Off in the distance, shrouded in mist and falling rain, Megan looked to see the sharply pointed steeple of the great stone church rising out of the water. Now it looked small, like a child's toy. It was impossible to believe that the water had covered this massive building, one of the largest in Johnstown!

Brian nodded. "I think you're right, sir. And that's on the corner of Franklin Street, so—" he looked around, "yep, I think you're right. This must be Kernville."

He peered in the opposite direction. "And look . . . look, sir . . . isn't that the hill across Stony Creek from Kernville?"

Ahead of them loomed the dark bulk of the mountain. And they were drifting steadily toward it!

5

5:03 P.M., *Friday, May 31, 1889*

Septimus Shaw took a pair of steel-rimmed glasses from his shirt pocket and carefully fitted them to the bridge of his nose. He peered through the soupy twilight.

"If we keep our present drift," he announced, "we ought to be able to reach the hillside."

"If we could only find something to use as an oar," Brian began, glancing around.

"That timber is much too heavy," declared Mr. Shaw, indicating the rubble floating around them. "We'll just have to keep a lookout for something suitable."

Megan moved nearer to the unconscious girl who lay so still and white. She took the wet shawl from her own shoulders and placed it under her head. Then she looked up at the boy and the old man in bewilderment.

"Can you tell me, please . . . what happened . . ." she asked in a halting voice.

Brian looked at her long and hard. Then he crawled across the wagon and sat down beside her. Unexpectedly, he took her hand. "I think the dam up at South Fork must have broken," he said quietly.

Megan nodded.

"I know about the dam," she said. "Papa and Mr. Morrell

and some of their friends were always worried about it. They went up a lot of times to check on it, I remember. . . ."

Fifteen miles above Johnstown, in the mountains, a group of wealthy men from Pittsburgh had bought a large tract of land with a lake and formed the South Fork Hunting and Fishing Club. They had rebuilt the old, existing dam to enlarge the lake and had built summer homes along its shores.

No one in Johnstown knew much about the mysterious club, for outsiders were warned off by fences and signs and guards. But the townspeople always lived with the dread and half-formed fear that sometime the dam might break. If it did, the water from the artificial lake would come crashing down the narrow valley that led to the town, just like a giant sluiceway. It was one of those curious things that people live with in fear, like the people who live beside a volcano, not really believing that disaster can happen to them.

"I went up there once," Brian said, "with a bunch of fellows, friends of mine. We wanted to see what it was like, and we wanted to fish."

Mr. Shaw had joined them, and he looked at Brian.

"What happened?" he asked.

"Well, this fellow with a gun came along and told us to get out. He said it was private property and we were poaching."

Brian gazed around the group.

"That was some place," he continued. "They had a sailboat on the lake! Imagine, a sailboat in the mountains! And big houses with porches all around them, and a lot of ladies walking around with parasols—oh, it was some place!"

"Did you see the dam?" Septimus asked.

"Sure did. There was even a little road across the top of it for the carriages to go over."

Just then there was a soft moan from the girl lying beside them.

Megan, who was nearest, bent over her. The girl's eyelids fluttered. "Oh . . . oh . . . what. . . ."

Gently Megan brushed back a strand of wet hair from her forehead.

"You're all right," she whispered softly. "You're safe. Don't worry, we'll take care of you."

The girl struggled to sit up and then sank back again. "Oh, my leg . . . it hurts. . . ."

"It will be all right soon," Megan said.

As she was speaking the words she was wondering how she could be saying this. She only knew that, somehow, she wanted to comfort this unknown girl. And she trusted, in some deep part of her, that Brian and Septimus Shaw would take care of all of them. She looked at Brian. "Do you suppose we could make a splint?"

He shook his head. "Not now. Not here. We'll try to get on land somewhere." He leaned over the girl. "What's your name? Where are you from?" he asked softly.

"Finley," the girl breathed. "Lottie Finley. My pa's got a little farm up above Woodvale."

"Yes . . . well, now," Septimus Shaw began, but before he could finish what he was about to say he was interrupted by shouting.

"Hey there—you on the raft! Somebody give us a hand, will you?"

They all looked in the direction of the voice.

Two young people were sitting astride a large, bobbing tar barrel, clinging to each other about the waist. Brian worked his way to the edge of the wagon, lay flat on his stomach, and extended an arm.

"Paddle a bit," he called to them, "and you can make it."

The young man on the barrel began to stroke the water using his arms as oars, and the young woman kicked with her feet. In a minute they had propelled the barrel alongside the wagon.

Brian gripped the young woman's arm and pulled her to safety. The man jumped as if he were playing leap frog and landed beside her. The wagon bed rocked with the added weight and then steadied itself.

For the first time Mrs. Alderson seemed to notice what was going on. She pointed to the young people.

"You'll kill us all," she screamed.

Mr. Shaw laid his hand on her arm. "Now, now, Mrs. Alderson," he said soothingly. "We're going to be all right. Very soon now we'll be on the hillside."

He looked at Brian and Megan and the two new people almost apologetically.

"She was visiting my wife when it happened. My wife is an invalid, and Mrs. Alderson had brought her some biscuits. She was looking out of the bedroom window and saw her own house break up and disappear. . . ."

Megan stared at him, sympathy welling in her.

"And . . . your wife?" she asked softly.

Septimus Shaw spread his hands in a strange, pathetic gesture. He shook his head.

To keep him from seeing the sudden tears that seared her eyes, Megan turned to the two newcomers.

They appeared to be about twenty and despite the dampness were jauntily dressed. The man was the most handsome Megan had ever seen—tall, with a crest of curling golden hair. The girl, too, was blond and pretty in a vacant-looking sort of way. Her blue silk dress had many ruffles and velvet bows.

"When we signed on with the road company," the young man said, "they promised us first-class railway coach for the whole tour! Nobody said anything about riding a barrel!"

He stuck out his hand toward Brian.

"Tom Hewitt, at your service! And Miss Daisy Cox—late of the *Night Off* company! Specialty: songs, dances, and comic patter!"

He gave the whole group an engaging crooked grin.

Daisy smoothed the wet ruffles of her spectacular dress. "I'm awfully pleased ta meetcha all," she chirped.

Brian was staring at her open-mouthed. Megan, near hysteria, fought to hold back laughter.

Once again she had the awful feeling of total unreality. She felt as if she were only dreaming that she was floating over a drowned city in the company of an odd assortment of strangers, with death and destruction all about them. Surely she would wake up soon and find herself safe and warm in her own home.

"We're going to try to get to the hillside"—it was Brian's voice, speaking to Tom—"and we'll have to anchor this thing somehow, until we can get the women off. . . ."

They had drifted to about a hundred yards of the mountainside, which jutted up before them like a huge muddy wall. Higher up on its flanks they could see a few scattered houses, with small groups of people standing about looking over the vast sea of destruction.

"It's going to be a rough go," Septimus Shaw said. "Look at that pile of wreckage!"

All along the edge of the mountain a dark crust of debris —timbers from buildings, uprooted trees, dead farm animals, and other only-guessed-at horrors—lay strewn about. It shifted uneasily in the treacherous currents, creaking and grinding.

"We've got to try before it's clear dark," Brian decided, "or we'll never make it."

He looked at Tom.

"One of us will have to go first and test it. The other will have to carry Lottie."

Septimus Shaw pulled himself slowly to his feet. Megan realized for the first time that he was a very old man, frail and fine-boned like a small gray sea bird.

"I will go first to test it," he said firmly. "I'm afraid I couldn't manage to carry anyone, and it will need two of you—she's a strapping big girl. . . ."

Brian was about to say no, but then he seemed to sense the old man's pride and dignity.

"All right," he agreed.

The wagon bed was wedged in a fairly solid manner against a pile of lumber. Since they had no rope to secure it or to secure themselves to one another, they decided that each would have to try it alone. Megan found herself closing her eyes tight and praying hard as Septimus took his first step from the safety of the wagon floor.

A second later, opening them, Megan saw him walking in the manner of all boys who cross a log over a creek—teetering from side to side with his arms stretched wide. He balanced delicate as a high-wire dancer. The lumber under him shifted a little, but being so tightly packed, it held firm. After what seemed an eternity he finally reached land and, grasping a young tree root, pulled himself onto a small ledge on the steep mountainside.

"Hurrah!" shouted Brian, waving. "Good for you! How was it?"

"Not bad," Septimus called gleefully. "Not bad at all. Quite sound really, must be very thick. I'm sure the ladies can make it if they're careful. It's slippery, though. . . ."

Brian turned to Megan. "You want to be next?"

She wanted to say no, I want to stay with you, but the way Brian was looking at her she knew she must do as he said.

She swallowed hard. "All right."

"Good girl!"

He held her hand as she made her first, tentative step onto the pile of debris. It gave a bit under her weight, like stepping into deep meadow grass.

"Take it easy now," Brian warned, letting go of her hand. "Don't hurry, and you can make it."

Megan, once started on her treacherous journey, gave no thought to the group watching her from the wagon or to Septimus Shaw on the shore. Her sodden skirt tied high about her waist, and barefoot, she picked her way carefully across the mud-jellied boards and along the roughened bark on the trunk of a giant oak tree, concentrating only on the next step ahead.

A peaked roof of what once must have been a hen house jutted in front of her like a small hill. She climbed carefully across and over the wet shingles and finally, with a desperate leap, touched solid earth. She felt Septimus' hand grip her and pull her upward to the ledge. From the wagon she could hear the cheering of her companions.

Daisy came next, light and agile as a dancer, and was pulled up to join them in record time. But Mrs. Alderson was another matter entirely. She flatly refused to leave the wagon. Megan could hear Brian entreating her, and Tom joined in the pleas.

"I'm too heavy," she kept wailing. "I'll sink . . . I know I'll sink. . . ."

Brian, who had been attempting to lift her to her feet, suddenly let go of her arms. She landed with a soft splat on the wagon floor.

"All right, you stupid old biddy," he shouted, his eyes blazing, "stay here and drown then. . . ."

Megan sucked in her breath.

"Oh, how awful!" she murmured, turning to Septimus for help.

"Can we . . ." she began, but he paid no attention to her, straining to watch the drama being played on the wagon.

Brian whirled around to Tom. "Come on," he said crisply, pointing to Lottie, "you take her feet, and I'll take her shoulders."

Mrs. Alderson scrambled to her feet. "Wait," she cried. "Wait for me."

Brian paid no attention to her. He was kneeling beside Lottie, saying something to her softly. Tom looked on.

Megan stood up and waved as the middle-aged woman began her wobbly crossing.

"Come on, Mrs. Alderson," she called. "You can make it! It's really pretty solid to walk on—just come slowly. . . ."

6

Darkness covered the drowned city. Through it fell a thin rain, but the little group from the wagon, huddling close together on the mountain ledge, was already so wet they scarcely noticed it. Lottie mercifully had again fainted from the pain of her perilous journey and lay still as death, her head cradled in Megan's lap. The rest sprawled exhausted on the rock.

Slowly they became aware that above them on the mountainside small, scattered fingers of yellow light pointed up through the murky gloom. Off to the left somewhere the sky was stained red, as if a gigantic fire were burning, though they could see no flame.

They could hear the creaks of the shifting mass of debris in the water and an occasional snap of timber breaking up, but there was no human sound at all.

Brian slowly hauled himself to his feet. He pointed toward the specks of light.

"There are a few houses up there," he said. "I'll go up and see if we can find some help."

Tom scrambled up. "Count me in," he said.

"The rest of you wait here until we get back," Brian directed. "Move about a bit if you want to keep warm. But be careful you don't slip."

Brian and Tom melted away into the darkness. With their going Megan felt fear return. A small sob escaped her. Suddenly she felt a hand grip hers.

"There, there, my dear. You've been such a brave girl this far," Septimus spoke quietly. "Don't give up now."

She was surprised at the strength of the old man's grasp. "Now tell me," he said, "just how it all happened with you."

So Megan found herself telling him about the attic, and going down to untie the dog, about the ducks and the pansies, about her father's coming, and Tim and Aunt Ella in the linen cupboard. As the words came tumbling out she found herself becoming herself again, an identity. No matter what else, she was still Megan Maxwell. She had lost everything, perhaps, but not that. Somehow it was very important.

Septimus Shaw listened gravely as the jumbled story unfolded. Megan clutched his hand more tightly.

"Do you think," she asked, "that they're all right—my family?"

"Well," he answered, smiling, "you're all right, aren't you? So it stands to reason. . . ."

"I think Papa made it to the hill," she agreed, "and Fanny and Louisa were already there. And Tim and Aunt Ella— why they probably were washed out of the house, like I was. . . ."

"So there, you see . . ." he began.

"Oh," Megan cried, "but I must find them."

"Of course," he agreed, "but not tonight, my dear. Not in the dark. Tomorrow will be time enough for that."

"Why, they're probably hunting for me now," she said eagerly.

"Yes, yes," he agreed.

Just then they heard footsteps and saw by the pale gold

gleam of two swinging lanterns Tom and Brian making their way carefully down the mud-slick slope. Two shadowy figures followed them.

"Halloa there," Brian shouted. "Good news! We've got help!"

They had brought two men from a house halfway up the mountain. Between them they carried a rough wooden door, apparently hastily torn from a shed.

"This will make a stretcher to carry Lottie," Brian explained. "The rest of us will have to walk, but it's not more than half a mile or so."

It was a tricky business on the narrow muddy ledge to lift the unconscious girl onto the makeshift stretcher, but they finally accomplished it. The two strangers started off on the steep climb with their awkward burden.

"There's a house up there," Brian told them, "and it's bursting its seams with people. The folks who live there have been taking in survivors for the past hour. The only room they've got is in a little shed outside, but they said we could stay there for the night. At least it will be dry."

He was helping Mrs. Alderson to her feet.

Megan felt herself lifted lightly.

"Come on, sweetheart! Old Uncle Tom will take care of you."

"Hey, what about me?" piped Daisy.

"Oh, you, luv—you might look dainty as a swan, but you're tough as an ox," Tom said lightly.

"Oh, get on with you," she laughed and scrambled to her feet.

Brian had been standing near the side of the ledge holding his lantern high. Suddenly they heard him gasp.

"Hold on a minute!"

They all turned to look.

At the far end of the ledge a large boulder jutted out of

the hillside. On its top, in the pale watery light of the moon, they saw the head of a child.

For one horrible moment it looked as if it had been severed and lay as on a plate.

"Good Lord!" exclaimed Septimus.

Two enormous blue eyes beneath a thatch of yellow hair watched them solemnly.

Still clutching the swinging lantern, Brian leaped toward the boulder and began to climb its slippery sides. The group watched him in silent disbelief.

"It's a boy," he called faintly. "He's alive."

He gathered the child under his arm like a sack of corn and maneuvered his way carefully down the steep spur of rock.

Gently he set the boy on his feet on the ledge. They were all looking at him in wonder, as if he were a being from another planet. He was nearly naked. A few tattered shreds of cloth hung from his thin white shoulders, his little hands were torn and caked with drying blood, and his face was incredibly dirty. He looked about six years old.

Brian knelt down in front of him.

"It's all right, fella," he said softly. "You're all right now. What's your name?"

The child did not speak. Not the slightest flicker of expression crossed his face. He just stared at them.

"Lord knows how long he's been up there," Brian said. "There's no one else that I could see. He was all alone."

"We must take him with us," Septimus said. "He's probably too frightened to speak. We can find out later. . . ."

Brian turned to Megan. "You take charge of him," he ordered.

"But . . ." she began to protest and then stopped. "Oh, all right."

She ripped off her outer skirt, more ashamed of the child's

nakedness than her own state of undress, and wrapped the damp folds about his thin little body. He made no movement, just stood there like a small stone statue.

"Come on," she said, grasping his tiny cold hand.

And so, slipping and straining through the darkness, they began to climb the steep hillside. Brian led the way, and the rest followed the bobbing dance of the lantern.

After what seemed an endless time of toiling through acres of mud, the shape of a house loomed up before them, its windows glowing with lamplight. A woman wrapped in a shawl came out on the porch and called to them.

"I'll show you where to go."

She led them to a small shed a few yards from the house.

"I'm sorry," she said, "that you'll have to stay here for the night. The house is full up, and there are four people hurt real bad who need the beds."

"This will be fine," Brian said. "We're just glad to have some place in out of the rain."

"I put down clean straw and tied the goats outside," the woman went on, "and there's hot food. I'll bring it down to you."

"What about Lottie—the girl with the broken leg?" Septimus asked.

"We got a woman in there"—she nodded toward the house—"who knows somethin' about doctorin'. She'll set it, and we'll keep her in the house. I made her a bed on the floor."

"We are very grateful to you," Septimus said.

"Pshaw, ain't nothin'. Just wish we could do more! Now, you just rest yourselves, and I'll bring you some eats."

Megan looked around the crude little shed. The floor was covered knee deep with fresh dry straw, and beside the door, neatly folded, was a pile of worn quilts and thin woolen blankets. Brian hung the lantern on a nail in the wall. It threw its wan light over the small room.

Megan looked at the little boy whose hand lay limp and cold in hers. He moved when she moved, stopped when she stopped; otherwise he might be dead.

"Come on and lie down," she said and pushed him down into the straw. She got one of the quilts and wrapped him in it, pulling the other corner over herself. It was so heavenly to be out of the chilling rain. The others took blankets and curled up, gratefully burrowing into the warm straw.

A few minutes later the woman appeared again, carrying a huge kettle in one hand and a stack of plates in the other.

"This'll do for starters," she said. "Ain't much, but I've got a batch of bread in the oven. It'll be ready shortly."

She ladled a thick stew of chicken and vegetables onto the plates and handed them around. They steamed in the chill air, sending up a marvelous fragrance.

For the first time, Megan realized that she was famished. She began to spoon up the rich gravy eagerly.

Then she felt the slightest stirring at her side. The child was staring at her plate. Megan hesitated. She could never remember a time when she had been so fiercely hungry as now. Almost slyly she glanced around. The others were busy eating, concentrating on themselves and paying no attention to her.

Looking away from the boy, she took another bite. Then suddenly, vivid in her mind's eye, she saw Timothy and heard his clear little voice say, "Look, Megs, I made a parade."

With a quick roughness, she handed her plate to the little boy. He made no move to take it, only looked at her with those enormous blue eyes.

"Here," she said, "open your mouth."

Still no movement.

She leaned over, parted his lips with her finger and thumb, and thrust a spoonful of stew into his mouth. The child hesitated a moment, then chewed and swallowed. Megan fed him another spoonful. And so, together, they finished the portion.

Only then, glancing up, did Megan notice Brian regarding her with an odd, unexplainable look.

7

When they had finished eating, Brian gathered up the plates and the empty kettle.

"I'll take these back to the house," he said.

The warm food and the dry, sweet-smelling straw cast a sort of drowsy spell over the little group. They burrowed deeper under the blankets. No one spoke. Each seemed to be lost in his own private thoughts, as if separately trying to come to some sort of understanding of what had happened before it could be translated into words.

A short while later Brian reappeared. He entered the shed quietly and sat down beside Megan.

"Hold out your hands," he said.

She obeyed. A small cry escaped her. She looked at them in amazement, as if they belonged to someone else. Her hands were cut and crusted with blood.

"Let's fix these up first," Brian said.

He had brought a pitcher of warm water, a tin of salve, and some clean strips of cotton torn from an old sheet. Gently, he bathed her hands, applied the soothing ointment, and bound them.

"Now, that's better," he said.

"I hadn't even noticed," Megan said. "I guess I must have hurt them climbing out of the house. . . ."

Brian turned his attention to the little boy. The child sat unresisting as Brian sponged the dirt from his face and bandaged the long, deep scratches on his arms and legs.

Megan leaned nearer.

"What's your name?" she asked.

The child made no reply.

"He doesn't speak English."

Megan was startled to hear Mrs. Alderson speak for the first time since they had left the wagon.

They all looked at her in surprise.

"How do you know that?" asked Megan.

"Because he's one of the Novak kids—at least I'm almost sure he is. There's a great brood of 'em, and I'll never be able to tell you which one he is. There's a new one every year! They all look alike, and they all have outlandish names. . . ." She looked at Septimus. "They live way down at the far end of our street. Polish—the dad works in the mill. All the Polacks look alike, and don't none of 'em speak English."

Septimus came over and looked down at the child. He laid his frail old hand on the tousled head.

"Yes, well . . . I don't really know," he said as an expression of tenderness crossed his face. "So—we will give you a name. We'll call you—Stefan! That's a fine, brave name for a fine, brave lad."

Megan had never known any Poles. They were part of the "foreign element" in town, people who had come to work in the steel mills. They lived jammed into tiny frame houses and died there among their own strange customs. Their lives never touched people like the Maxwells, and so to Megan they were somehow not real. If they existed at all, it was only as a sort of shadowy background to the life of Johnstown as she knew it.

"Stefan!" Brian's voice interrupted her thoughts. "Yes, that's a good name."

There was still no flicker of expression on the child's face, so they had no way of knowing whether or not he understood them.

"It's unnatural," Septimus said softly. "If only he would cry."

Brian rocked back on his heels and surveyed the group. "I was talking to a bunch of men up at the house," he said, "and they're starting a search party. I'm going with them."

He looked at Tom. "You come along, too?"

"Sure, why not."

Stretching, Tom stood up.

"We'll have to know just who is missing from each of us, and from where," Brian said, "so we'll have something to go on. What about you?" he asked Septimus.

"There's only my wife, Bess." The old eyes glazed. "She has been bedridden for years and helpless. I just don't know. . . ." Then he straightened his shoulders. "I am a watch-maker. I have a small shop on Birch Street, and we live above it. When the . . . the water hit . . . we were on the second floor, Mrs. Alderson, my wife, and I. The whole place just seemed to . . . crumble. We were standing by the window, I remember, and that wagon seemed to be lodged against it. I don't know where it came from. I remember crawling onto it and pulling Mrs. Alderson out, and then I started back for my wife, and then . . . there was nothing . . . the house was just . . . gone. . . ."

He was trembling all over. They looked at him in horror and pity.

"Well, sir," Brian said finally, "there's a good chance her bed might have floated free. Don't worry, we'll find her for you."

Mrs. Alderson began to cry. "I saw it go," she wailed, "my house—everything!"

Brian said to Septimus, "Does she have a family?"

"Only her husband at home. He's an engineer on the railroad. He went out to work early today—he's on the Altoona run."

"Likely then he wasn't even in town," Brian said. "He's probably all right somewhere."

Megan had been listening to all of this, her mind running in crazy circles. Brian turned to her.

"What did you say your name is?"

Megan looked at him in astonishment. It seemed to her that she had known him all of her life, and here he was, asking her name!

"M-m-Maxwell," she stuttered.

It was Brian's turn for surprise.

"The store—Maxwell and Foster?" he asked. "That's your dad?"

She nodded.

"Then you live in that big brick place out on Franklin Street?"

Again she nodded. It was the showplace of Johnstown.

"Holy mackerel!" he breathed. Then he recovered himself. "All right, how many in your family?"

So again she told her story. "Mama and my sister Grace are with my grandparents in Kansas City—my grandpa is ill. And as soon as Fanny and Louisa were better—they had the measles—well, Mama and Grace left," Megan explained.

"So, then, there's your dad and your sisters, your aunt, and your little brother," Brian said.

"Oh, and Hulda—there's Hulda, too. She's our cook."

Brian scratched his head. "I hope I can remember all of this," he said.

Tom was looking at Megan with a curious expression. "Don't you worry, sweetheart," he said. "Uncle Tom will find them for you."

Daisy had sat up and was brushing off wisps of straw.

"While you're about it, Tom Hewitt, you just might look for my trunk," she said. "All those beautiful dresses—cost me a year's wages!"

Tom laughed. "Now there's a woman for you! Well, come on. Let's get this show on the road."

"Be careful, lads," Septimus said with a worried frown, "and come back to us. . . ."

After Brian and Tom had left, the others settled down into the deep straw, pulling the blankets close around them.

"You know, this reminds me of the time we were playing one-night stands, way upstate in New York," Daisy said drowsily, "a bunch of dinky little towns, and we traveled by wagon. The horse went lame way out in the sticks, and we had to sleep in a barn. Oh, that was years ago. . . ."

Surprise flitted across Septimus' face.

"Why, child," he said, "how could you remember 'years ago'?"

"Oh, I've been on the stage since I was three," she said and added proudly, "My mum and dad were on the boards. We're a real theatrical family."

Megan was fascinated. She had never met an actress. Her parents thought stage people were a showy and disreputable lot, and she had never been allowed to go to the theater.

"Isn't it scary," she asked, "to get up on a stage, in front of people like that?"

"Scary? Sure it is! But, oh, it's grand—the lights and the music, and all the people clapping, and everyone loving you. And the pretty clothes!"

She pulled the blanket up to her chin.

"I do hope Tom finds that trunk," she mourned. "There's this one dress—oh, it's so elegant! Red silk, and all this gold lace. . . ."

"What about the others in the company?" Septimus asked.

"Oh, they're all right," she said. "We were on the train, see—we're playing Altoona next. We got on the train this morning, and then they kept holding it up, saying the tracks was washed out. Well, we waited and played cards and fooled around, and then around four o'clock this man, he comes busting into the railroad yard on a train going backward and yelling for everyone to get off and run."

Her eyes grew wide, remembering.

"My, that was a scramble! Me and Tom were the last at the door. I saw everyone running up a hillside there, and then suddenly there's this water all around. There was a big barrel floating by, and Tom, he snared it, and we climbed on."

She giggled softly. "It was like riding horseback. Me hanging onto Tom, and off we went."

Megan thought about Tom. Nobody had ever called her sweetheart before! Why, he was even older and handsomer than Will Alford. Kit's party seemed ages and ages away. . . .

"Have you known Tom long?" she asked shyly.

"We just met up a couple of months ago, with this company," Daisy said, her eyes alight. "Ain't he handsome, though?"

"Well," Septimus said, "I think we had all better try to get some sleep now, until the lads come back."

Megan snuggled down into the straw. It felt prickly against her face. Her long lace-trimmed drawers and her petticoat had begun to dry and clung stiff and clammy to her legs. Her bandaged hands hurt.

A sense of terrible desolation washed over her, and she had to bite her lip to keep from sobbing aloud.

8

Megan stirred uneasily at the weight pressing against her. Opening her eyes sleepily, she became aware of Stefan curled close, his head on her shoulder. His breathing was quiet and regular.

She pulled away from him in irritation and sat up, rubbing her eyes. The shed was in semidarkness, but she could see humped shadows where the others lay sleeping. She had no idea of the time or how long she had been asleep.

Cautiously and without a sound, she groped her way to the open door of the shed and stood there, absently brushing the wisps of straw from her wrinkled petticoat.

The rain had stopped, but the air was heavy with mist. Off to the right she could see a few lamps were still burning in the nearby house, but she could see no other signs of life. Suddenly through the stillness came, clear and true, the sound of a bell.

"Bong . . . bong . . . bong. . . ."

Eleven times the mellow chime poured through the mist. She knew that sound, had heard it every hour for years: the great bell on the Lutheran church tower—a familiar thing! A small surge of warmth went through her.

Just then she heard a soft "baah"!

Peering around the corner of the shed, she saw two goats tethered to a stake. She went over and touched their warm, heaving flanks, and they nuzzled her like friendly puppies.

A tall shadow loomed out of the fog so suddenly that it startled her.

"Oh . . ." she cried softly.

"Shhh! It's only me, Brian."

He was standing beside her, tall and comforting.

"Are you all right?" he asked anxiously.

"Yes," she whispered. "I just couldn't sleep. I'm so glad you're back. Where's Tom?"

"I don't know. Are the others asleep?"

"Yes. . . ."

"Come over here a ways, so's we won't waken them."

They crossed the yard to a small bench beside an old grape arbor. Off to the right Megan could see the sky brightening with light. It puzzled her.

"I heard the bell tower chime eleven," she said, "and yet, look, it's getting light! What's happened, Brian? Is it day or night?"

"It's night," he replied grimly. "That light is from a fire." He gripped her hand so hard it hurt.

"Oh, Megan," he said, "I never saw anything like it! It's at the bridge—you know, the big stone railroad bridge over by the Cambria Iron Works. It must have held, and . . . stuff . . . has piled up there—it looks a mile high—and it's—it's all burning. . . ."

"Oh, no!" she gasped.

Now she could see, filtered through the fog, even at that distance, huge tongues of flame eating the sky.

They looked at each other in silence.

"And, Tom—" she faltered finally, "where. . . .'"

"Oh, he's all right, I think. We separated after a bit,

thought we'd have a better chance of finding someone. He'll be fine; he can find his way."

She was half afraid to ask. "And you—did you find anyone?"

"You wouldn't believe it," he said. "There are people everywhere, all over the hillside here. They're even sitting in trees, some of them. And some are just walking around! We're lucky to have the shed."

"Oh, Brian. . . ."

"I kept asking everyone—" His voice broke, and he fell silent.

In that moment Megan knew that this boy, who had been so strong and cheerful, the one all of them had depended on, was frightened and lonely, too. Funny, she thought, I might have lived all my life and never met Brian O'Meara. For though the town was small, the social strata were firmly defined. There were so many levels of existence layered so neatly that they never touched each other. Suddenly this realization seemed crazier than anything that had happened to her this night.

With a quick, selfless grace, Megan took his hand and held it.

"Brian," she said softly, "tell me about yourself."

Looking at him in the uneasy halflight, she could see his eyes seem to retreat somewhere inside of himself, as if searching for a past that went beyond this dreadful day. She could see his broad, open face streaked with dirt, black hair tangled and unkempt, his clothes torn and damp, his shoes mud-caked. He slumped in weariness.

"There's not much to tell," he said finally.

There was a long silence. She still held his hand in her own with no trace of self-consciousness.

"My mum and dad have a little grocery store," he said. "Or at least they did have. . . ."

His eyes went dark with remembering.

"Not much of a store, really, but a living. And getting better every year. My mum's a careful manager. There's just the three of us, you see, and I work there after school and summers. Dad had got him a horse and rig, and we were going to start a delivery service this summer."

Brian's voice was growing stronger.

"I'm going to college," he said with pride. "I finished high school this year, and we figured if we got the delivery business worked up, in a year I'd have saved enough money. I'm going to Pittsburgh, to the University Law School."

He stopped suddenly.

"Or, I *was*," he added ruefully.

"You will," Megan said. "I know it."

"I guess I'm here because of that horse and rig," he mused. "The water had been coming up all day. Folks kept coming into the store all day and buying up supplies, and we were so busy we didn't have time to notice much how high the water was getting.

"Dad and I had built a new barn out back of the store early in the spring. We rigged up a door in the roof to let out heat in the summer and to air the place out.

"Well, along about four o'clock, Dad got to worrying about Princess, our new mare, and he told me to go out to the barn and check on her and to move the feed sacks up to the loft, so they wouldn't get wet and spoil.

"There hadn't been any customers in for a while, and Mum says, 'We'll close early this evening and eat supper.' We live upstairs, over the store.

"So I went out to the barn. It's high, and the water hadn't reached there yet, but I knew it was higher than it usually gets, and it might come in this time. So I started carting feed sacks up to the loft.

"There's a little window up there, faces the house, and when I heard this big, roaring noise I went over and looked out. My dad was leaning out of the upstairs window, and he yells at me, 'Don't come over, stay where you are. . . .' "

He fell silent again. Megan waited patiently.

"Then I saw our house go over," he said in a flat voice, "just like that. . . . It just . . . went. I could feel the barn break up under me. I made a dive for that door in the roof, and got through it, and just hung on. . . ."

"And then what happened?" asked Megan.

He shook himself.

"Well," he continued, "I just rode that roof like a raft. I don't remember much until it crashed into a building. There was a window, and I climbed through, and there were all these people in there—the women were crying and praying and carrying on something terrible. . . .

"You know, I do remember something strange. I looked at my watch, and do you know how long the whole thing took?"

She shook her head.

"Ten minutes! Only ten minutes!"

She stared at him in disbelief.

He reached into his pocket and pulled out a round, flat watch, turning it slowly in his hand.

"I just got it, for graduation," he said. "I remember, I looked at it when I went to the barn, and it was seven minutes past four. So you see, I knew exactly what time it was."

He held the watch to his ear.

"It's stopped ticking. Water has got to it, I guess."

"I'll bet Mr. Shaw can fix it," said Megan. "He's a watchmaker."

"Maybe," Brian said doubtfully.

"But go on," she urged. "What happened then?"

"Oh . . . well, I went to the window where some of the men were standing. And that's when I saw you."

"Me?" she cried in wonderment, and then, "Oh, yes . . . yes?"

"Well, you looked so . . . so pitiful, crouched there on that soggy mattress, and so scared. You didn't even call out or cry or anything. You just looked at me like some kind of hurt animal. And I thought, well, I just thought I had to help you."

He looked at her solemnly.

"I'm glad I did," he said.

It was Megan's turn for remembering, how the building he had left was smashed by the railway car and disappeared in the swirling water.

"So am I," she said quietly.

They sat without speaking for a while. The light from the distant fire stained their faces with a ruddy glow. Finally Megan spoke.

"In the morning I'm coming with you. And we'll find our families."

"I think we'd better try to get some sleep now," Brian said. "Tomorrow will be a long day."

They stood up and made their way along the muddy path toward the shed. All about them the night was filled with ominous sounds. Although it was nearly a mile away, they could hear a faint crackling from the huge fire at the stone bridge, and its unearthly light swelled and diminished, shifting the shadows.

From below in the town came the crunch of great timbers moving in the water. Somewhere a dog was yelping, a frantic, harried note. The two goats stirred restlessly on their tethers. Megan shivered in the chill, damp air.

9

6:30 A.M., *Saturday, June 1, 1889*

"Here's some coffee for ya," called a strong, cheerful voice.

Reluctantly Megan pulled herself up from a deep well of sleep. She rubbed her eyes and sat up.

Gray, featureless light filled the little shed, showing the humped bodies sprawled closely together in the straw. In the doorway stood the woman of the night before, holding a steaming granite coffee pot.

The others slowly pulled themselves to sitting positions.

We must look like crazy people, thought Megan, seeing the others, rumpled and wild, with straw clinging to their uncombed hair and wrinkled clothing.

"Food's runnin' a mite low, but I got griddle cakes comin'," the woman went on. "You just drink this and then come on up to the house."

She thrust an assortment of chipped china mugs and tin cups at them and began pouring the coffee.

Megan cupped her cold hands about the mug, grateful for its small warmth. She felt stiff and sore and very cold. This time Stefan did not have to be fed. He gulped the hot, strong brew greedily.

Glancing about, Megan met Tom's eyes. He was smiling at her.

"Oh," she cried in surprise, "you're back! I never heard you come in."

"You were all sleeping sound as the dead," he began and then checked himself. He took a quick swallow of coffee to cover his ill-made remark.

"It was pretty late," he finished lamely.

Brian was looking at him. "You find out anything?" he asked.

Tom shook his head. "Not much," he mumbled, as if reluctant to speak in front of the others. Brian seemed to understand.

"This coffee sure tastes good," he said and then added, "I wonder what time it is, anyway?"

Tom pulled a watch from his pocket and consulted it. "Quarter to seven, on the nose."

Megan was staring at the watch.

"Oh," she said, "what a beautiful watch! May I see it?"

For a fraction of a second Tom's eyes narrowed. Then he handed it to her.

"Fellow gave it to me last night," he said, "for helping him. He was caught under a pile of lumber and I pulled him out."

Megan turned the watch over in her hand. It was large, and the gold case was heavy with carving. The porcelain face was adorned with a smiling sun face, the points of which formed a compass decorated artfully in enamel of soft rose and blue and gilt.

"Why that must have been Mr. Horace Fitch," she said in amazement. "This is his watch."

Tom's face grew tight.

Megan looked wonderingly at the group.

"He's Papa's good friend," she explained, "and he's often shown me this watch. I'd know it anywhere. He bought it in

Switzerland, and he's so proud of it. And I know his son, Charley. . . ."

"Well," Tom said, beaming, "now then, I'm happy I could help a friend of yours."

Megan handed back the watch.

"Where did you find him?" she asked eagerly. "Was he hurt bad?"

"Hurt? Nope. Once I got that lumber off him he was fine."

"I'm so glad! Do you remember where he was?"

Tom shook his head. "I couldn't say. Even if I knew the town, which I don't, everything looked the same in the dark."

Megan scrambled to her feet.

"We've got to find him again," she cried. "Maybe he's seen Papa. . . ."

Brian stood up.

"Wait," he said. "The lady said she had some breakfast for us. We'd better eat first, and then we can start out."

Megan felt a pull at her petticoat. Stefan was clutching the folds and looking up at her.

"Oh, all right," she said impatiently. "But let's hurry!"

The others joined them at the door of the shed, and they stepped out into the chill morning light.

Later, each person in the little group would remember this morning, June 1, 1889, in a different way. Some would tell that it was sunny, and some would say it was raining, but everyone would agree on one thing.

The silence.

It was uncanny, unearthly. It was a silence so deep it could be touched. It filled the whole mountain valley and reached its cold, inhuman fingers down into the heart.

Morning sounds that everyone took for granted, sounds so

customary they ceased to be noticed, were absent. The voices of a family at breakfast, children calling to each other, the school bell, a wagon clattering over cobblestones, the bark of a dog, the train whistles that were so much a part of life in Johnstown—all were silent.

Actually, the day was neither sunny nor rainy. A pewter-colored sky hung low over the hills furred in spring green, and in the valley where the town had been patches of mist drifted here and there.

From the hillside where they stood they could see the valley spread out before them, but it was a place they no longer knew, a place of unimaginable desolation.

Only a few buildings were still standing: the great stone Methodist church, the Baltimore and Ohio railroad station, the school on Adams Street. Alma Hall, where town meetings were held, and the Union Street School were still where they ought to be. The blackened rafters of St. John's Church were sending thin ribbons of smoke to the sky, but a hundred feet away, where the great Maxwell mansion had stood, there was nothing but a pile of rubble.

Whole houses were crazily tilted, parts of them sheared off as if by a giant knife or turned completely upside down.

The two rivers, swollen and choked with debris, churned toward the stone bridge. Elsewhere brown water lay in great greasy-looking lakes.

Railway cars, wagons, dead farm animals, uprooted trees lay helter-skelter everywhere.

And on all the hillsides surrounding the town were small knots of people huddled against the chill morning and locked in the silence of shock as they surveyed the ruined city. They were looking at the very face of hell.

The little group stood quietly. Yesterday had been filled

with terror. It had been for each of them purely a matter of survival. It had possessed a kind of awful majesty of its own, God's own most dreadful majesty with its threat of total destruction and the single sweet miracle of life.

But this crushed and broken body of a whole city was incredibly sordid and heartbreaking.

They looked at each other, stricken in disbelief. How long they stood silently they did not know.

Finally Septimus spoke. "Let's go to the house."

Without a word they crossed the muddy yard and climbed the porch steps.

As they entered the kitchen Megan was aware of the great number of people there. There must have been twenty crowded into the little room. Women and children were seated at a long, narrow table, and the men stood, eating from plates they held in their hands. The woman who had brought them coffee stood beside the coal stove, her face ruddy with the heat.

"Oh, here you are," she called, waving a pancake turner at them. "Come on in an' grab a plate."

Several of the women who had finished eating stood up.

"Come on, dear," one of them said to Megan. "You just set down here with your little boy."

Megan looked at her in astonishment. Stefan was still clinging to her skirt.

"He's not my little boy . . ." she began, but before she could finish, she found herself seated, with a plate of griddle cakes thrust in front of her.

As plates seemed to be in short supply, reluctantly she allowed Stefan to eat from hers. Again, he did not need to be fed. Well, she thought, at least he knows how to eat.

There was not much conversation. It was as if the shocking sights they had witnessed so far and the fear of what they might discover had struck them dumb. They ate mechanically, for the most part unaware of what they were eating.

When she had finished, Megan carried her plate to the wooden sink board. As soon as she rose from her chair, Stefan was beside her.

"Go and sit down," she whispered to him fiercely.

He made no move. His fingers gripped her skirt more tightly.

Exasperated, she turned to the woman at the stove.

"Do you suppose he can stay here with you?" she asked desperately. "I've got to go and try to find my family, and I can't have him tagging along."

The woman looked at her curiously. "Doesn't he belong to you?"

"Oh, my goodness, no!" Megan replied. "We don't even know who he is—we found him on the ledge last night."

The woman gazed down at the child with compassion.

"Why, sure," she said. "He can stay here till we find his folks. Poor little mite!"

As she reached out her hand toward him, Stefan drew back, cowering. He hid his face in the folds of Megan's petticoat.

The woman smiled. "Seems like he's got other ideas."

She bent down.

"Come on, little fella. You come along with me now."

Stefan drew back farther, and his body stiffened. The woman stood up.

"Looks like you've got yourself a boy," she said and turned back to the stove.

"Oh, no! He just can't come . . ." began Megan. She tried to loosen the child's fingers.

Suddenly Brian was at her side.

"Megan," he said softly, "listen, he's scared. We'll take him along with us. Someone might recognize him."

She looked at him helplessly.

"He won't be much trouble," he went on. "And besides, it looks as if we don't have any choice."

"Oh, for heaven's sakes . . . all right then! Come on!" she said, grabbing Stefan roughly and heading for the porch.

The people from the house were drifting about aimlessly. Some sat on the porch steps, some stood in small groups in the yard.

They saw Septimus Shaw at one end of the porch. He was standing before a wooden bench that held a basin of water, and in front of a cracked and smoky mirror he had propped up he was carefully shaving his face.

Megan regarded him with amazement. He finished and began to clip his neat little gray beard. Then he stepped back, smoothed his wrinkled coat, and surveyed them solemnly.

"I'll get you a fresh basin of water," he said to Megan, "and you may borrow my comb."

Megan suppressed a wild desire to laugh. In the midst of such disaster, he was concerned about his appearance.

"I haven't got time . . ." she began.

"Of course you have time," he said firmly. He tilted the basin over the porch railing and refilled it from a tin pitcher. "And wash the child, too. His own mother wouldn't recognize him."

When Megan caught a glimpse of her own reflection in the mirror, she was appalled. Septimus was right. Her own father wouldn't know her, with her dirt-streaked face, her tangled hair, and her bedraggled petticoat.

And so Megan, who was used to the privacy of a huge bathroom, with soft linen towels and scented soaps, stood

meekly on the crowded porch and washed herself. She also scrubbed Stefan. The little boy was still wrapped in her skirt. He looked ridiculous.

"Do you think," she called over her shoulder to Septimus, "that the lady might have a little pair of trousers for him? He can't go about dressed like this."

"I'll ask," Septimus said and vanished into the house.

A few minutes later he reappeared with some rough pants and a shirt.

"They'll be too big," he apologized, "but it's all she's got."

Megan dressed the unprotesting child in the overlarge clothes, rolling up the cuffs and sleeves, and pulling the comb through his tangled curls. He did not wince or make any sound.

Then she carefully combed her own long dark hair and tied it with a ribbon from her bodice.

Suddenly she felt immeasurably better.

10

7:30 A.M., *Saturday, June 1, 1889*

Brian and Septimus had gathered the group together
again at the doorway to the shed. Because of their shared
experience they had become, in a curious way, like a little
family, having nowhere to belong and no one else. Megan
and Stefan joined them.

"The lady says we may use this shed as long as we need
it," Septimus was saying, "and I think we should make it our
headquarters until we can make other arrangements."

Suddenly his thin frame was racked by a cough.

"You're right," Brian agreed, "and I think you should stay
here."

He glanced at Mrs. Alderson, who leaned against the shed
wall, bedraggled and bewildered.

"I don't think she should go traipsing about, sir. And if
you could sort of look after her, we'll hunt for her husband
and your wife. And we'll report back here."

Septimus considered this. "Well," he said, "perhaps you're
right. I don't feel quite up to a lot of walking. . . ."

Again a spasm of coughing shook him.

"Wouldn't you like to stay here, too?" Brian said to
Megan. "I'll look around for your folks. . . ."

"No," she replied firmly. "I'm going with you."

"But . . ." he began.

"Brian"—Megan's voice was clear and strong—"I'm not a child! I know it's horrible down there . . ."—she gestured toward the town—"but I'm going with you."

"Well . . . all right," he said.

It was Daisy's turn to speak. "And I'm coming, too. Tom and I ought to try to find the rest of the company. I know they got to that other hill."

She turned to Tom. "The next show is to be in a place called Altoona. If we can find à way to get there. . . ."

Tom was looking at Megan.

"I think we ought to try to help her . . ." he began.

"Well," Brian said, "we'll all stick together for a while and see what we can find out."

"Just don't forget us," Septimus pleaded.

"Oh, no, sir. We won't. We'll report back here, we promise."

And so they began to make their way carefully down the steep hillside in the direction of town. It was treacherous going, for underfoot the mud was slick as grease. Slipping and sliding, they finally reached the bank of Stony Creek.

Swollen and choked with all kinds of debris, it raged along its downward course toward the great stone railway bridge. From that bridge they could see black smoke billowing from the fires still burning there. All other bridges had been washed away.

"I don't see how we're ever going to get across," Brian said in dismay.

"Look—down there!" Megan cried.

Farther down the bank they could see three men. They were busy working at something.

"Hey, there!" Brian called, waving.

They made their way cautiously along the steep slope. One of the men waved back.

"We're tryin' to make a raft," he said, as they came closer. "My family is over there, and I got to get to them."

"We'll help," volunteered Brian. "We want to get across, too."

Megan, Daisy, and Stefan sat on a fallen log, while Brian and Tom joined the men.

"We ain't got no tools," one man said, "but we fished out this coil of rope from the water, and we figured we might lash some boards together. Just enough to get 'er across."

Nearly an hour went by as they worked, and no one spoke much. Across the stream Megan could see small groups of people emerging from the few buildings still standing. They seemed to be wandering about aimlessly in the debris-choked, muddy streets.

Far on the other side of town Green Hill loomed. That was where her father had carried Fanny and Louisa. Though the distance was nearly a mile, she could see faintly what looked to be movement there, as if a giant anthill were stirring.

Finally Brian, Tom, and the other men stepped back and stood looking down at the flimsy raft.

"She don't look like much of a craft," one of the men said.

"As long as it will make two trips, just to get us all across," Brian said, "it'll have to do. I'll go over with you first," he said to the men, "and then bring it back for the others."

They had found among the piles of lumber jammed at the stream's edge a few small boards to use as oars.

"You wait here," Brian told Megan, "and I'll be back."

They steadied the gimcrack raft in the wicked-looking

water, and the three men climbed aboard. Brian gave a mighty shove and leaped on.

Megan closed her eyes tight and prayed as she had never prayed before. When she opened them, she could see that the flimsy little raft had nearly reached the town side of the stream. It was only about thirty yards across, but the current was moving swiftly, and trees and parts of buildings were still being carried along with it, making a dangerous obstacle course.

With a shout the men landed on the town-side bank. Brian waved gleefully across to them.

"You go on down a piece," he called. "The current has carried her downstream. I'm starting back for you."

The men steadied the raft as he climbed aboard again and shoved him back into the water.

Megan, Stefan, Daisy, and Tom scrambled along the slope while watching anxiously. Brian manipulated the makeshift oar, propelling his way carefully around the floating debris. Once he struck against the branches of a tree. Moving with it, the raft drifted farther downstream.

"It's caught underneath," Tom shouted. "Reach down and push against that big branch."

Frantically striking with his oar, Brian pushed against the entangling branch. The raft teetered sickeningly, and then, with a shriek of wood against wood, pulled free and righted itself. The tree drifted on past, and Brian paddled madly. He pulled up against the shore. Tom grabbed the raft to hold it.

Suddenly he lost his footing in the slippery mud. He fell flat, being pulled toward the water.

"Grab me!" he screamed.

Megan flung herself on top of him, clutching at his trouser leg.

"Hold me!" she shouted to Daisy, as she felt herself slipping toward the water.

Brian, at the edge of the raft, managed to grip a sapling that hung over the bank. With the combined weight of the three of them they were able to steady the raft and get the end of it pulled onto the shore. They sat on the muddy bank, gasping for breath.

Daisy bent double, giggling.

"Ohhh . . . you look like three pigs in a mud wallow," she chortled.

Suddenly anger flashed through Megan, hot and fierce. She jumped to her feet, her eyes burning.

"Oh, you make me sick!" she cried. "I didn't see you doing anything to help!"

The smile drained from Daisy's face. She looked at Megan in astonishment.

"Come on, now! I didn't mean anything by it."

"You're just . . . disgusting! You stand there in your fancy dress and call *me* a pig!" Megan shouted.

And then all her held-in terror and loneliness cracked open, and she broke into uncontrollable sobbing. She simply stood there, white and shaking, tasting the bitter salt of her own tears.

Then she felt strong arms about her and her face being pressed against a hard shoulder.

"There, there, sweetheart," Tom soothed her, "don't cry. . . ."

He held her close against him until the shuddering sobs finally subsided.

"Now, then, that's better." He tilted her face up to his, and with a soiled and damp handkerchief he wiped away her tears.

Megan felt too hollow even to be ashamed. But a lifetime

of learning good manners could not be denied. She turned to Daisy, who was looking at her curiously.

"I'm sorry," she said.

Daisy's smile was immediate and good-natured. "That's all right," she said. "I didn't have no call to laugh."

Brian, who had watched the whole scene with a stony face, said quickly, "Well, come on, now. Let's get across."

With Tom steadying her, Megan climbed onto the wobbling raft. Brian lifted Stefan on beside her and helped Daisy to clamber aboard. Then he gave a great shove to push the raft away from the bank and leaped to join them.

With the two boys paddling, their crossing was quicker and easier than before. The men who had built the raft helped them ashore on the other side.

"We'll just leave 'er here," one of them said, tying an end of the rope to a heavy plank that lay on the shore. "Then if you need to get back, it'll be here. No sense wasting all that work."

11

10:15 A.M., Saturday, June 1, 1889

For years afterward Megan would waken in the night, cold and shaken, finding her pillow wet with tears. She would relive in nightmare this day. When she was a very old lady and her grandchildren asked her to tell them the story of the Johnstown Flood, her eyes would grow bleak with memory.

"I can't really tell you all of it," she would say. "It was too horrible for any words."

At the shed on the hillside and while they were building the raft, it had seemed the most important thing in the world just to get down into the town and begin searching for their families. But now that they were actually here, standing amid the incredible ruin, they felt a deadly numbness steal through them. All about them was desolation so great they simply did not know where to begin.

Finally Brian broke the silence.

"We'll just have to stay together," he said in desperation. "Nothing looks familiar anymore. If we separate we might never find each other again."

He looked across the open acres of mud and the huge piles of wreckage, some as high as twenty or thirty feet, mountains of broken buildings piled crazily, with vast pools of water between.

Megan was trying valiantly to push down the deep despair that threatened to engulf her.

"If we can just get over to Green Hill," she faltered, "and find Papa, he'll know what to do. . . ."

"All right," Brian agreed. "That's a beginning."

He looked at the others. "Do you agree?"

"Sure thing," Tom said. "Your papa is a pretty big man in this town, isn't he?"

"Yes," Megan said. "I guess he is."

"Well, then, he's the one to find first," Tom stated.

Brian had climbed up on a pile of wreckage and was looking around him.

"I can't tell just where we are," he said, "but I guess the best thing to do is just head toward Green Hill. It's hard to find where a street was. . . ."

They began to make their way across the ruined city. It was necessary to walk carefully, for danger lurked everywhere. The deep mud made each step a gigantic effort.

They were forced to detour around piles of boards and bricks that had once been houses. Pathetic remnants of daily living were strewn all about them—bicycle wheels, chamber pots, broken dishes. A bedraggled doll with one blue china eye and a stained pink dress floated in a pool of water. Parts of chairs, beds, cooking pans, sodden books, kerosene lamps, a smashed violin—all lay helter-skelter.

"Oh, my God!" gasped Daisy.

She had stopped, frozen in terror, pointing.

From a pile of rubble that had once been a house, half exposed beneath the falling beam that had killed her, lay the body of a woman. Her arms were outstretched as if seeking help, and her long hair fell loosely, covering her face.

"Oh, no!" Megan cried.

She felt Brian's hand on her arm.

"Don't look," he said sharply. "We can't help her now."

Megan felt her stomach heave. She pulled away from Brian. "I'm going to be sick," she mumbled.

Turning away, she knelt in the mud and threw up.

Everything swam in front of her. When the dizziness had ceased finally, she stood up, clenching her hands tightly together.

"I'm all right now," she said faintly. "I'm sorry. . . . Let's go on. . . ."

She became aware of Stefan at her side. On a sudden impulse she bent down and kissed the top of his head, hugging him close. "It's all right," she whispered. "Come on, now. . . ."

They saw many more bodies that day, men and women and children. And in the course of that terrible journey they learned to avert their eyes and blank out their minds against these poor creatures who were past any help. Megan wept only once more that day, later on in the afternoon when she saw the small feathered body of a duck drowned in a little pool.

Strangely, everywhere there were living people, singly and in small groups. Some were climbing out of partly crushed buildings or picking their way among the debris. Their faces were expressionless, like sleepwalkers. Sometimes they stopped to pick something up, turning it over in their hands, and then dropping it again listlessly. Most of them seemed to move without direction, not knowing where to go. There was no crying, and almost no one spoke. It was a nightmare world, totally unreal.

A woman, white-faced and wild-eyed, approached them.

She snatched at Stefan, who was clinging to Megan's hand.

"Billy . . . Billy . . ." she cried.

She dropped to her knees beside him and took his face in her hands. A look of slow bewilderment filled her eyes.

"You're not my little Billy," she said in a broken voice, shaking her head from side to side.

Before they could say anything, she had wandered off to another group of people.

"Come on," Brian said gruffly. "Let's keep going."

By some curious miracle the mechanism of the great bell on the Lutheran church had been undamaged, and it continued to ring out the hours. They heard ten strike, and then eleven, as they made their way across the town. Every person they saw they stopped to ask, "Have you seen Mr. Edward Maxwell?"

"Have you seen Mr. and Mrs. John O'Meara?"

"Do you know this little boy?"

"Have you seen Bess Shaw or Henry Alderson?"

And always the answer was the same.

"Sorry, no . . . never heard of 'em."

"Sure, I know Mr. Maxwell. You his girl? Well, I'll tell him I saw you if I run across him."

Megan asked for Timothy and Aunt Ella, for Hulda, and for her girlfriend Kit, for John Huber and Will Alford. Yet with all the people they met that morning, she did not see a familiar face.

They had reached a point in their journey where the way seemed completely blocked. An enormous mountain of wreckage stood in front of them, and on either side of it the water lay too deep to wade through.

"Do you think we could climb over?" Megan asked.

Directly in front of them a house lay on its side. A huge tree had been driven completely through it, like a giant skewer, pinning it sideways to the ground.

Brian approached cautiously and peered through a broken window.

"Sounds crazy," he said, "but I think we might be able to crawl through the house if we're careful. I can see right through!"

The others joined him.

"Let me go first to test it."

He took a piece of board and broke the remaining jagged shreds of glass from the window frame to allow passage and then carefully crawled over the frame.

"Seems solid enough," he called from inside. "Sure kind of weird, though—I'm walking on the wall. . . ."

The rest followed him. It was such a strange sensation. Inside everything was completely topsy-turvy. The furniture was piled in a heap in one corner, and curtains still hung at the windows. On the side wall, now beneath their feet like a floor, pictures still hung, some with the glass unbroken. They had to step over them carefully.

"I feel like Alice in Wonderland—" Megan said, "like I've gone through the looking glass."

"Well, I never heard of that," Daisy said, "but it really feels . . . queer-like!"

They crossed two rooms in this fashion and could see light ahead through another window. Brian, who was first, peered out.

"The way the house is tilted it's a good ten-foot drop to the ground. It looks clear ahead, but I'm not sure we can get out of the house."

"Maybe we can find some rope," Tom suggested.

They were in what had been the kitchen, standing almost knee-deep in broken crockery, pans, spilled flour, and salt and beans.

"Wait a minute!" Megan said. "I think there were some curtains with heavy tiebacks in the living room. Could we knot them together and make a rope?"

"Good idea," Brian replied. "I'll go and see."

He began to crawl back toward the other room.

"Hey, look here!" cried Tom.

He reached down into the mess at his feet and picked up an unbroken Mason jar full of canned peaches.

"Food!" he exulted and wrestled to open it.

"Would we dare?" Megan asked.

"Why not? I don't know about the rest of you, but I'm starved. Breakfast seems a mighty long time ago. And this will be safe to eat—the water didn't get to it."

He managed to get the jar open and handed it to Megan. Gingerly she reached in with her fingers and took out a juicy chunk of fruit. She handed it to Stefan.

"Here," she said, "eat this."

The child accepted it without a word. When Brian returned they were all licking the sweet juice from their fingers.

"Don't worry, we saved you some," Daisy said, grinning.

Brian was carrying four heavy braided silk tassels with long fringe.

"These ought to do," he said.

While he finished off the peaches, Megan and Tom tied the silk ropes together.

Brian and Tom braced a heavy table against the wall by the window and tied the makeshift rope securely. It dangled to within four feet of the ground below.

"You'll have to be careful," Brian warned.

He lowered himself out and down.

It was no problem for Daisy to follow.

"I used to climb the stage curtain ropes when I was little," she remarked cheerfully.

But for Megan it was a real trial. Her bandaged hands burned as she tried to grip the slippery silk cord. She winced with pain.

"I don't think I can hang on," she cried.

"Yes, you can," ordered Brian from below. "It will only hurt for a minute, and then it will be over."

Finally she did it, white and shaking, biting her lip to keep from crying aloud.

Tom was the last one down, hanging on with one hand and carrying Stefan with the other. As he leaped to the ground they heard a snap as the silk rope broke loose.

"Well," Brian said with a wry smile, "at least there was one bit of luck."

The way ahead was mucky but fairly open. But by the time they had gone only a short way their feet and legs were so heavy with mud they could hardly lift them. Each step made a sucking, slapping sound. Even though the day was chill, Megan felt sweat trickle down her face.

At last she gasped, "I'm going to have to rest for a while—I'm so tired!"

Just at that moment, from a pile of timbers off to one side of them, they heard a mad, wild yelping.

"There's a dog caught in there," Brian said.

Megan was staring at the pile of lumber with a strange expression. Then she began to run toward it, awkwardly slipping in the deep mud. She started to pull at the boards. The yelping grew louder and more frenzied.

"Senator! Senator!" she cried. "Good boy . . . good boy. . . ."

Brian was at her side, flinging away pieces of wood.

In a few seconds a sleek black head appeared. The dog was mad with delight. He leaped on Megan and knocked her down, licking her joyously. She sat in the mud, laughing and crying.

"It's our dog," she kept saying over and over.

Senator's shiny coat was mud spattered, and a long, blood-crusted gash cut across his flank, but he seemed to have no broken bones. Finding him was one of those curious miracles that arise from disaster, something wholly without probability, something that just happens. From that moment on, the big dog never left her side, walking with his nose touching her skirt.

12

12 Noon, Saturday, June 1, 1889

It was Tom who made the next find on their strange journey. He had been in the lead, when suddenly he stopped and let out a long, low whistle.

"Look at this," he said softly.

They had come to a fence that by some fantastic quirk had withstood the flood. There, caught against the pickets and among the sodden shrubbery that lined it was—money!

Wet and stained but unmistakable—dollar bills, and fives and tens. Silver dollars and dimes lay scattered about among the paper money.

Almost unaware of the others, Tom knelt and began to gather it up, stuffing it into the pockets of his coat.

"By golly," he chuckled, "a real honest-to-gosh money bush!"

The others watched him in amazement.

"Hey," Brian said, "what are you doing? That doesn't belong to you!"

It was Tom's turn for amazement. He lifted his head briefly and looked at them.

"What do you mean? I found it."

"Yes, but—"

"What do you mean—but? It sure doesn't belong to anyone else."

He was scrabbling now on his knees in the mud, scooping up the money as fast as he was able.

Brian gazed at him in stony silence for a moment. Then he turned his back and walked rapidly away.

Megan stood forlorn. Finally, hitching up her skirt and clutching Stefan's hand, she plodded through the mud after him.

"Brian, wait for me," she called.

She was panting when she finally caught up with him.

"I can't go so fast. . . ."

He stopped then, and reaching down, he lifted Stefan and set him on his shoulder. He began to walk again more slowly but without speaking. Glancing back, Megan could see Tom still gathering up the sodden money. Daisy stood quietly beside him.

"Brian," said Megan, "it really doesn't belong to anyone, not now, I mean. How could anyone know who it belongs to? Tom probably has never seen that much money in his whole life."

Brian made no reply.

"It's not as if it were . . . stealing."

He stopped and looked at her. His eyes were cold. "Isn't it?" was all that he said.

Then he turned his back and walked on.

Megan followed dispiritedly. In her whole life she had never really thought about money itself. There was always plenty. The comforts and beauty it could buy had always been a part of her everyday life.

But thinking about Tom and the precarious life of an actor, she could understand his greed. Brian was being intolerably stuffy. She looked at the uncompromising set of his shoulders, where Stefan perched like a little bird. The longer she thought about it the angrier she grew, until finally she could hold back no longer.

"I think you're being awfully . . . self-righteous," she flared.

He stopped and spun around to face her. His eyes were blazing.

"Listen, Miss Megan Maxwell," he said angrily. "What you think doesn't concern me at all! There are things that are right and things that are wrong, and whether you're rich or poor, or fat or thin, or whatever, it doesn't change it.

"So you can feel sorry for Tom Hewitt, or any other thing you want to feel, but it still doesn't make his taking that money right in my book. I don't care if every living person in Johnstown is doing it—it's still *not* right!

"So you can think what you want to think—that's your business. But what I think is my business, see?"

Megan was astonished at his fury. She stood looking at him for a moment. No one had ever spoken to her in such a manner.

Finally, drawing the shreds of her dignity about her, she said haughtily, "All right! From now on I'll keep my opinions to myself. You don't have to worry!"

"I'm not worried," he replied shortly and walked on.

They continued in miserable silence. When Tom and Daisy finally caught up with them no word was spoken about the money.

It was after two o'clock when they reached the corner of Jackson and Main streets, where Megan's home had stood. As they approached it, she made no sound at all.

There was nothing there.

The stately house of rosy brick, with its green lawns, great trees, flower beds, and stable, had vanished completely. A few bits of ragged timber and broken brick lay in a sea of mud.

Megan stood unmoving.

She felt a cold numbness settle over her body. Senator, sensing something amiss, whimpered. Absently Megan stroked his silky head.

The others had no words for her. There was nothing to be said. They stood together, huddled and forlorn.

Two blocks away, across a field of rubble, they could see a tall brick building still standing, almost intact.

"That's the Adams Street School," Brian said. "Let's go over and see if there's anyone we know there."

He seemed to have forgotten his anger, for very gently he took Megan's hand and led her away. She did not protest but moved along with him like a sleepwalker. She did not look back.

As they approached the school a tall man in a torn coat waved to them.

"Hey, young fellows! Come here a minute!"

Drawing near, through shock-glazed eyes, Megan recognized the man—Captain A. N. Hart, a friend of her father's. His was the first familiar face she had seen the entire day.

Desperation drove the numbness from her mind. Pulling away from Brian, she ran to the man and grasped his sleeve.

"Oh, Captain Hart," she cried in a broken voice, "it's me, Megan Maxwell!"

He looked at her almost curiously, from haunted eyes.

"Are you one of Edward Maxwell's girls?" he asked finally.

"Yes . . . yes . . ." she cried. "Have you seen my papa?"

He shook his head sadly.

"No, girl. Sorry. . . ."

Then, seeing her stricken face, he patted her hand as if she were a small child. "Don't worry, my dear. I'm sure he's all right. He'll find you. . . ."

He turned away abruptly, but not before Megan saw

tears glisten in his sunken eyes. She felt all hope drain from her.

Captain Hart was speaking to Brian and Tom.

"Some of us are getting a meeting organized. Could you boys scout around and round up every able-bodied man you can find? If we're going to get anything done we'll all have to work together."

Having received instructions to be back in half an hour, Brian and Tom went off in different directions.

Captain Hart turned once again to Megan.

"You and the other young lady just come inside and rest awhile. You look plain tuckered out. Meanwhile, I'll just ask around—find out if anyone has seen your father."

He led them up the steps of the ugly old building. They walked past haggard men who kept coming and going, and Captain Hart led them into the first empty room.

Megan had never seen the inside of the Adams Street School. She had been taught at home by a governess and then had gone to the Washington Female Academy, a finishing school for young ladies.

The big, dingy room felt warm and good. There were lists of spelling words and sums on the blackboards, and everything smelled of chalk dust and coal and wet wool. The teacher's desk stood on a raised platform at the front. On it stood a vase of pink roses, drooping now, their petals scattered on the scratched and battered wood.

Daisy claimed the chair.

"I'll be teacher," she said.

Megan settled Stefan at one of the small desks and sank down beside him. Wearily she put her head down on her folded arms. Nothing seemed to matter much anymore. All she wanted to do was rest.

13

3:00 P.M., *Saturday, June 1, 1889*

By three o'clock that afternoon the schoolroom was filled with men. Megan, Daisy, and Stefan had moved to a corner at the back and sat quietly watching them come in singly and in small groups.

They were all white-faced and silent, unshaven, many with their clothes torn and stiff with dried mud. Any who talked did so softly, their expressions serious. Megan searched each face in vain, hoping against hope to see her father.

Brian and Tom came in at last and, seeing the girls, joined them in the corner. Brian slid onto the bench beside Megan. Fumbling in his pocket, he produced three withered apples.

"A man gave me these," he whispered. "One for you and one for Stefan and Daisy. Go ahead, eat."

Megan was so hungry by now that even the dry and bitter fruit was welcome. She chewed and swallowed even the musky core.

Captain Hart finally entered the schoolroom and stepped up to the platform. All the low talking ceased, and the faces of the men packed in so closely turned to him in expectation. Captain Hart's tall body straightened, and his voice rang out strong and clear.

"Fellows," he began informally, "it seems to me that the first thing we've got to do is to elect a leader, someone to be in charge of everything. If we're going to get anything done, we've got to work together and not go repeating our efforts.

"Now, I'm going to nominate Mr. Arthur J. Moxham. You all know Mr. Moxham as a fine businessman with a good head on his shoulders and a good organizer of men."

"Hear! Hear!" called several men from the crowd, and a small splatter of applause broke forth.

A vigorous-looking man with well-brushed brown hair and a neat beard stood up and made his way toward the platform. His lively eyes surveyed the room.

"I thank you men for your confidence"—his voice had the mellow lilt of the Welsh tongue—"and I'll do my best to serve all of you and our town."

The whole room burst into a faint cheering.

"Now then," he continued, raising his hand, "there's no time for speeches. A heap of work is to be done, and the sooner we get on with it the better.

"As I see it, our first problem here is the dead, for fear of the chance of epidemic. And I'm asking the Reverend Chapman and the Reverend Beale to be in charge of this."

The two ministers stood up, grave and pale.

"You'll see that a temporary morgue is set up—here in the school to start with, as they're already bringing bodies in here. And you will see to proper identification and decent burial."

He glanced around the room.

"Any doctors present?"

Two men stood up.

"Ah, yes—Dr. Lowman and the other gentleman. Mighty glad to see you! We'll need a hospital for the wounded. You find a suitable building and gather what medical supplies you can find.

"Charley, you and Bert, you get some crews together and begin to clear some streets so that wagons can get through. And Bill, you round up all the foodstuff that's fit to eat. Take it to the Methodist church and give it out as needed.

"Each of you take a room here in the school and sign up your volunteers."

His clear voice continued giving crisp orders. Men who had been listless before now began to talk together quietly and shift restlessly. Now that there was something for them to do they seemed to come alive again.

"Captain Hart here will deputize men for police work. What property that is left has got to be protected.

"You will all report back here at least once a day to let me know what you are doing and what your problems are. That way we can coordinate our work. Is that understood?"

And so, in less than an hour, and less than twenty-four hours after the city had been destroyed, this astonishing group of men had set to work to clean up the wreckage and to rebuild.

The schoolroom was suddenly empty. Brian looked across the heads of the two girls at Tom.

"I think we'd better get the girls back to the shed before dark. Then we can come back and volunteer."

"Well, why don't you just do that," Tom replied. "I think I'll stick around here for a while."

"But, Brian," Megan protested, "I want to go on looking for Papa. . . ."

There was a kind of desperation in Brian's voice.

"Megan, listen! It will soon be dark. There's no place for you to sleep and no food. You just can't stay here. Don't be so doggone stubborn all the time. . . ."

He grabbed her roughly by the arm.

"Now, *come on!*"

With Stefan clinging to her skirt, Megan found herself being dragged forcibly across the room. She was really furious now, twisting and wrenching to free herself from his grip.

"You let me go," she shouted. "I can look after myself. I don't need you and your bossiness! Let go of me, Brian O'Meara!"

They had reached the hallway. Brian stopped so suddenly that Megan careened into him. She pulled away and darted into the hall, only nearly to collide with two men who were carrying a door between them like a stretcher. On the door lay the body of a young man.

Megan stopped still in horror. Then she clutched the sleeve of one of the stretcher bearers, her face sick and white.

"Is he . . ." she asked in a whisper.

"Dead, miss," replied the man, a look of compassion on his face. "Is he a relative of yours?"

Blindly Megan put her hands to her face and turned to Brian. He put his arms about her and held her close. No tears came, only a violent shivering which she could not stop.

"That was Will Alford," she gasped, hiding her face against Brian's coat, feeling the rough wool scratch her cheek. "I was at a party, and he was there—John Huber's friend from Princeton, and I wanted him to dance with me, but he only asked me once and I wanted to make him jealous and so I flirted with Charley Fitch, only he never even noticed me, and now . . . now he's *dead!*"

Megan looked up at Brian.

"Oh, Brian . . . take me away from here . . . *please!*"

The dreadful journey back across the drowned city was made almost in silence. They had started the day in fear, but also in hope. And now, exhausted and defeated, they dragged themselves wearily through the rubble.

They had found no one belonging to them, and they had no word of consolation for the two they had left behind.

They had even lost one of their party. Tom had drifted off down the hallway of the schoolhouse to join a group of men, melting away from them with only a vague farewell.

"I'll keep in touch . . ." he'd said.

Even stouthearted little Daisy was listless with despair, tagging along in silence.

The small raft lay where they had moored it. It was completely dark now, with only a faint ugly red light from the stone bridge, where a few fires still doggedly burned. They were too tired to be frightened as they pushed off into the sluggish stream.

It was a tricky crossing, for Senator kept shifting about and the raft floated dangerously low. In the dark, things kept bumping against it, and several times it spun completely around, caught in the rush of an eddy. But finally they reached the hillside.

The climb up the slippery mountain path was torture. Weak with hunger and exhaustion, her legs aching against the pull, Megan stumbled after Brian, half carrying and half dragging the sleepy child. Through this whole day he had made not a single sound, not even a whimper. They had reached the conclusion that he was deaf and dumb. But now Megan was too dispirited to care. She hauled him along without a word.

As they approached the shed they could see a slight shadow against the dim flare of the kerosene lamp. Septimus Shaw stepped out to greet them.

"Oh, my dear children," he cried, his voice breaking. "I am so glad to see you safely back!"

Taking Megan's arm, he helped her through the door and settled her down in a pile of straw. It was deliciously warm and dry and sweet-smelling.

"I have been so worried," he went on, "and when dark came and you weren't here—yes, well. . . ."

His old voice trailed off, and he hastily brushed a tear from his bleak gray eyes.

"Har-um, well . . . now, I'll just get you some food. A farmer came by this afternoon with a wagonload of supplies. Now, you just rest and I'll. . . ."

He bustled out without finishing the sentence.

"He really does care about us," Megan said wonderingly. "I guess we're all the family he's got now."

The unspoken words hung in the air: *He* may be the only family we have now.

Septimus returned presently from the house with a platter of fried ham, fresh bread, and coffee. At first there was complete silence as they ravenously wolfed down the food. Nothing had ever before tasted so marvelous to Megan. Even small Stefan ate with obvious enjoyment.

When they were blissfully filled, they began to tell Septimus of the day's adventures. He listened gravely, shaking his head from time to time and murmuring his comments.

"Well, we are very lucky to have food and shelter here," he said finally. "After you left this morning about twenty more poor souls came drifting in. They had spent the night in the open and were in a dreadful state.

"When the farmer came by with his wagon, he took a number of them up to his place. There just wasn't any more room here."

"And Mrs. Alderson," Megan asked. "How is she?"

Septimus smiled. "Just fine! She's a good sort really, you know. She turned to and is up at the house helping with the cooking. Having something to do was all she needed to brighten her spirits a bit.

"And I," he went on with some pride, "I have been learning a new trade—doctoring! I've been helping the lady take care of the sick. Our little Lottie is doing as well as can be expected. We put a pretty passable splint on her leg, if I do say so myself!"

Megan burrowed herself deeper into the straw. She could hear the voices of Brian and Septimus droning on, but the words began to run together with no meaning.

Senator, smelling wet and doggy, curled close to her, his cold nose against her arm. Stefan lay with his tousled head in her lap, his soft breathing regular and easy. Megan pulled the old quilt closer around all of them. And with a small sigh, she fell asleep.

14

8:30 A.M., Sunday, June 2, 1889

They had all once again washed themselves at the tin basin on the porch of the house, taken turns eating breakfast with strangers, and were now gathered at the shed door. A strangely assorted little family, they had lost Tom and added Senator.

"Oh, Tom'll look after himself all right," Daisy said philosophically. "That kind always does. I've met a lot of fellows like Tom, not so handsome maybe, but alike inside. They come and go. They're lovely, but you can't count on 'em. Now that he's got that money he found, he'll be off somewhere."

"But what about you?" Megan asked. "What will you do?"

Daisy smoothed the sagging ruffles of her blue silk skirt. "Well, if I can just get to Altoona and meet up with the rest of the company, I'll be all right."

Megan thought about Tom. She thought about his golden hair, of how he had held her in his arms and called her sweetheart.

"Do you think Tom will be there?"

Daisy shrugged. "Who knows? Maybe, maybe not. I'll tell you what I miss more than Tom Hewitt, though—my trunk full of dresses! I'll never find a red dress like that one—never!"

It had been decided that Brian, Megan, and Daisy would return to the stricken town. Megan had been very firm.

"I *have* to go on looking," she said, "and nothing could be worse than yesterday."

But there was still the problem of Stefan, who refused to leave Megan's side. They knew he would not be able to make the journey again.

"I don't think he can understand—I don't even know if he can hear me," Megan said. "But I've got to try. . . ."

She knelt beside the small boy and took his thin face gently in her hands.

"Listen, Stefan," she said softly, "I have to go away for a little while. But I will come back for you—I promise! You must be a good boy and stay here with Mr. Shaw today. I will come back tonight; that's a promise."

The child looked at her intently with no change of expression. She bent forward suddenly and kissed his cheek. And just as suddenly he threw his arms about her neck and hugged her hard.

He made no struggle when Megan, her eyes blurred with tears, put his tiny hand in Septimus' and quickly walked down the path.

As they made their way toward the raft, Brian was making plans for the day.

"I was talking with some of the men in the yard this morning. They heard a rumor that a rescue train from Pittsburgh is due in today. They were working all night to fix the tracks that were washed out from Sang Hollow in to Johnstown. It seems to me that would be a good place for us to head. It's likely a lot of folks will gather there, and we might learn something."

So once again they rode the bobbing raft over into town. They began to pick their way through the now familiar rubble.

There were more people today, and they stopped each person they saw to ask the same questions over and over again.

"Have you see Mr. Edward Maxwell?"

"Mr. and Mrs. John O'Meara?"

"We're looking for an invalid lady—Mrs. Shaw."

Rumor was rampant everywhere. There were 10,000 dead! Men had gotten into whiskey barrels and were drunk and fighting! People were looting houses and stores! No one was safe!

The faithful bell of the Lutheran church boomed twelve before they reached the railroad yards, or what was left of them. But they had heard more and more stories of a train getting through, filled with food and clothing.

Many people were now hurrying in the same direction. Most of them had been without food for nearly two days, and many were injured. Almost everyone had lost all or part of his family, and all were desperate for news as well as food.

Tables had been hastily improvised from bits of lumber, and the food and clothing were being distributed from these. Bill Williams' supply crew was in charge, and things were being done in a surprisingly orderly manner. People were lined up, quietly awaiting whatever might be given them.

"You two stay here," Brian told Megan and Daisy, "and keep asking. I'll go back to the Adams Street School to check on a few things. Mind, you wait here for me and don't go wandering off!"

Megan knew, although he did not say, that Brian was

going to investigate the growing list of the dead. Suddenly she felt terribly alone and frightened. She kept a tight hold on Senator's collar.

More and more people kept gathering. Megan desperately searched each face for a familiar one. Stories were being circulated among the crowd of the horrors at the stone railroad bridge. The tremendous pile of wreckage that had built up had trapped hundreds of people when it caught fire.

Suddenly Daisy gave a shriek.

"Oh . . . it's Mr. Peterson!"

She grabbed Megan's arm and began to run toward a small cluster of people standing a few yards away.

"Mr. Peterson! It's me, Daisy Cox!"

She flung herself into the arms of a portly, red-faced gentleman.

"Daisy girl!" he cried, embracing her.

The men and women crowded around Daisy, all talking at once. Finally Daisy turned to Megan.

"Megan, it's my company!" she cried, radiant.

Megan forced a wan smile.

The portly man had his arm around Daisy.

"We've found a wagon to take us over the mountain to Altoona," he was saying.

"Oh, Megan," Daisy said, "why don't you come with us? We can take care of you till you find your folks."

"You're certainly welcome, miss," the man said. "You ought to grab at the chance to get out of here. . . ."

He gestured around at the tattered, hungry mob and the desolate ruins.

Megan shook her head slowly. "Thank you," she said, "but no. I've got to stay."

She thought about Brian and Mr. Shaw and Stefan.

"I promised."

"Well," Daisy said doubtfully, "I just don't like leaving you here all alone. . . ."

"Oh, I'll be all right." Megan forced a smile. "Honest. I'll just wait here for Brian."

"But suppose he doesn't come back?"

"He will," Megan said firmly, "and besides, it's different for me, you see. Johnstown is my home, and all my family are here . . . somewhere. . . ."

"Are you sure you don't mind my leaving?"

"No, really. You must go with your friends."

Impulsively, Megan stepped forward and threw her arms about Daisy.

"Good luck to you," she whispered against Daisy's cheek. "And I'm sorry for the things I said. I'm so glad to have known you, and I hope we meet again sometime. I'll come to see you on the stage. . . ."

Daisy returned the hug heartily.

" 'Bye, Megan. You're first-rate in my book! And I just know you'll find your folks. Tell Brian and Mr. Shaw I said good-bye."

Sadly Megan watched the little group hurry off together in the direction of Prospect Hill. She reached down and scratched Senator's head.

"Well, boy," she said, "it looks as if we're on our own for a while."

Megan continued to move about from one knot of people to another, asking and searching. Some of the sights she saw were almost comical. An old man with a long beard walked by her, dressed in a red flannel petticoat. A fat lady wearing an oversize pair of men's boots waddled along, bobbing up and down like a pigeon.

Twice Megan met acquaintances, but none had seen her father. Nearly an hour went by, and still Brian had not returned. More and more often Megan found herself turning to stare at a tall, dark-haired boy only to find a stranger. A small panic began to grow in her.

Suppose he doesn't come back, she thought. What will I do?

And then from somewhere near the edge of the growing crowd, Megan heard an amazing sound—singing!

"A mighty forr-tress iss our Gott,

"A bul-vark neffer fay-yel-ling. . . ."

Megan stood still, straining to hear. She could distinguish a strong voice leading, carrying over the others.

"Our helper He amid de flud

"Off mortal illss pre-vayel-ling. . . ."

Megan could never mistake that voice. She had heard it all through her childhood, a background to memories of a warm, bright kitchen, the smell of good food and furniture polish, scented soap—home!

Hulda!

Breathlessly Megan began to push her way through the crowd toward the sound. A cluster of people stood beside one of the tables where food was being handed out. And there, her broad, red face dirty, her starched apron hanging in tatters, stood Hulda.

In a moment Megan was enfolded in strong arms. Crying and laughing, Hulda kept kissing her over and over again.

"Ach, Miss Megan, Miss Megan! Gott iss gud . . . Gott iss gud. . . ."

For the next half hour, and frequently lapsing into German, Hulda talked without ceasing, stopping often to give Megan a bearish hug. Beside her, smiling and quiet, was her husband, Gus. They had found each other only an hour before.

Hulda and Gus, to their great sorrow, had no children of their own, and so they looked upon the Maxwells as their family. They had determined to go seeking them.

"And Tim and Aunt Ella—" Megan ventured, "you haven't seen them?"

Hulda shook her head sadly.

"Ach, Miss Megan, it vas all so . . . crazy-like! De house just . . . break up. I hang onto Master Tim's liddle wooden horsie. I can't remember nothings till I'm in de vader. Some mans, he come riding by on a roof, and he safe me. . . ."

Gus was standing over her, smiling.

"Don't you vorry, liddle von," he said to Megan. "Ve look after you now and find your papa."

Gus had been given some cheese and crackers from the store of provisions being handed out, and so the three of them, sharing with Senator, sat on a pile of boards to eat and make their plans.

Megan told them of all that had happened to her up until their meeting.

"Brian said he would come back," she told them, "and I know he will. And then there's Stefan and Mr. Shaw. I promised I would come back to them. So I've got to. You do understand, don't you?"

"Vy shure," Gus agreed, "you make a promise, you got to keep it."

"Dis vay, ve got more folks hunting for your papa. Such a big, fine man! I know he's safe," Hulda said. "Gus, he'll go up to Green Hill and find him."

And so it was decided. Gus started off, and Megan waited with Hulda.

The long afternoon dragged on, with more and more people coming for food and news and help. The provisions were running low, but rumor had it that another train was on its way. Pittsburgh had rallied, as well as all the little towns along the main line of the railroad. Some of the telegraph lines had been repaired, and a few wagons were able to get through the streets that had been cleared hurriedly.

But still Brian did not come. Megan found herself unable to sit still. She kept jumping up and searching again and again through the thickening throngs. Her head began to ache from looking into so many faces.

Suppose he had come and couldn't find her?

15

3:30 P.M., Sunday, June 2, 1889

The afternoon was waning. Megan, who usually loved the night, with the curtains drawn, the lamps lit, and the family gathered together, found herself harboring a growing fear. This night would be filled with phantoms lurking in the ruins.

She felt also a great restlessness.

"Oh, Hulda! I can't stand just sitting here, doing nothing! I can't stand just . . . *waiting!*"

"Now, now, Miss Megan. Vat gud it do you to go traipsing about? De Bible say vait . . . vait upon de Lord."

"But—" Megan began. She never finished the sentence.

A number of men and boys were carrying some boxes to the provision tables. Tousled, dirty, she saw a familiar face —John Huber!

"John—John," Megan called, running toward him.

"Hey, Megan!" John cried, his face opening to a smile.

"Oh, John—I'm so glad to see you! Is Kit all right?"

"Yes, she's fine. She's been so worried about you. Golly, this is great! Have you seen your father? He's been hunting you all day."

Megan grabbed his hands. "John! You've *seen* Papa?"

"Sure. We spent Friday night with him and your little sisters. We all got up to Green Hill before the flood wave hit town. He's been half crazy hunting you."

Megan was sobbing with joy.

"Oh, John! I've been hunting him everywhere. . . ."

"We're all staying with a family named Meade—it's a big white frame house with a picket fence up on Green Hill. You could go up there, I guess. They've been awfully nice. Our whole family went up there on Friday afternoon. But, Megan, I can't find Will—you know, Will Alford, my friend from college. He went in to town right after dinner on Friday to check on train schedules, and—"

Megan's happiness drained away suddenly.

"Oh, John," she said softly, "I'm so sorry. . . ."

"Have you seen him? Is he. . . ."

Megan nodded sorrowfully.

John looked at her for a long moment. Then he turned away and hid his face in his hands.

She could find no words to comfort him. She simply stood beside him in silence.

"Megan."

She heard her name spoken so quietly it was like the shadow of a sound. Turning around, she came face to face with Brian.

He was very pale. His tall body was stooped, and his eyes were dazed as if suddenly wakened from sleep. Her delight in seeing him fled swiftly. He looked so different from the boy she knew.

"Brian . . . what happened?" Her question was a whisper.

"I found my parents," he said tonelessly, "at the Adams Street School. . . ."

"Oh, no! Not. . . ."

"Dead," he said in a flat, terrible voice. "Both of them. . . ."

Later, Megan would never remember how the next hour passed. It was one of those dark places that her mind would refuse to enter, sealed shut forever.

She would recall, faintly, how they sat together on the pile of boards and ate the rest of the cheese and crackers. And that after a long while Brian began to talk of his childhood and all of the memories of his life with his parents.

They sat together in the midst of a shifting sea of people who drifted about them and never really touched them at all. The two of them made a small and lonely island.

Darkness fell. A damp cold crept in from the stagnant pools of water that lay everywhere. There were a few lanterns bobbing in the gloom, and here and there a small fire flickered, where a group of people huddled for warmth.

Megan raised her head listlessly as the church bell boomed seven.

She found herself looking into her father's face!

At first Megan just sat there, staring at him. She did not say a word. Then she felt herself gathered into his arms.

"Oh, my little girl . . . my Megan," he said brokenly, stroking her tangled hair.

All the gates of her misery broke open then, and she clung to him, sobbing as if her heart would break.

"Papa . . . Papa . . . Papa. . . ."

It was much later. Gus had returned and had built a small fire for them to ward off the numbing cold and the terrors of the dark. They sat around it, warming their hands.

They had shared their experiences of the past three days. Megan had told her father the whole story, and Brian had told of his loss. Mr. Maxwell in turn told of his agonizing search for his family.

"Louisa and Fanny were safe, and when I turned around I

saw you heading back for the house. I was frantic. I started
back, and then I saw that wall of water coming. There was
nothing I could do—I knew I'd never make it back to the
house in time. . . ."

Mr. Maxwell shook his head dazedly.

"I simply don't remember! I do recall taking the little ones
to John Meade's house, and then they told me that I wandered around all night, seeking you. . . .

"The next day I went to where our house had been and to
the store, and there was . . . nothing! I went to the telegraph
office to try to get a message out to your mother. I knew she
would be mad with fear and trying to get home.

"Only," and he shook his head sadly, "there is no home for
her to come to. . . ."

They were silent for a long moment.

"Well, I guess I'd better be starting back," Brian said finally. "I promised Mr. Shaw. . . ."

Megan's father put his hand on Brian's shoulder. He had
listened with deep compassion to the boy's story.

"Nonsense, my boy," he said, his voice gruff with emotion.
"You must come with us now. I can never express to you my
gratitude for the care you have taken of my girl. . . ."

He looked fondly at Megan.

"We will all go back to Green Hill," he continued. "I have
a friend who has graciously taken us in, and we can stay
there until we decide what to do. We must, at all cost, stay
together now. We still have to find Timothy and Ella. I have
every hope that, since Megan and Hulda are alive, we will
find them, too."

As she listened to her father's voice, firm and sure, taking
charge of things, Megan began to think her own thoughts.

And then she heard her own voice, almost as if it belonged to a stranger, small but also firm.

"Papa," she said, "I think Brian is right. We have to go back."

Her father stared at her, his eyes wide in the firelight.

"*We?*" he said incredulously. "What do you mean—we?"

Megan leaned over and took her father's hand.

"Papa," she said gently, "they're waiting for Brian and me. We promised we'd come back. If you could see Stefan, how little he is, and, well . . . I keep thinking of Tim, and how if he were all alone. . . ."

"But, Megan," her father protested, "I cannot permit you to go off like this. It is unthinkable! It is too dangerous in the dark, a young girl—" His voice broke. "Now that I have found you, I cannot risk losing you again."

Megan looked, really looked, at her father for the first time. During the past two days she had thought of him unceasingly. Her every effort had been directed toward finding him, this rock on which her whole life had been founded.

She saw his slim, spare neatness, heard his precise, clipped speech, thought gratefully of his inflexible rules of order and good behavior that were founded on love, rules that had made her whole life, though she had never been aware of it, warm and secure and happy. She had thought of him with love and longing, and never more than at this moment.

And beside him there in the flickering firelight was Brian, his head bowed.

Megan kissed her father's cheek.

"Papa," she said softly, "Brian will take care of me. And tomorrow we will bring Stefan and Mr. Shaw over to Green Hill. I told them you would know what to do and that you would take care of all of us."

Mr. Maxwell was still for a long time. He gave Megan a searching look. Then he patted her cheek and straightened his shoulders briskly.

"Very well, then," he said, "I think it is a foolhardy thing to do, but if you must . . . well, then you must. Gus and I will go with you as far as your raft and see you safely across the water."

It was agreed among them that Hulda and Gus would go back with Mr. Maxwell to Green Hill and that they would all meet at the provision train in the morning.

From somewhere Mr. Maxwell got a kerosene lantern. By this watery light they made their way to the bank where the raft lay moored. It was nearly midnight by the time they found it, for they had lost their way several times in the unfamiliar dark.

Senator refused to leave Megan's side as she stepped onto the rickety raft. Water sloshed over its sides.

"Don't worry, Papa," she called. "It's carried us across before. It will be all right."

"Take care," Mr. Maxwell called, lifting his lantern high. "We'll see you in the morning. . . ."

They reached the far shore and looked back across the stream, seeing the lantern lifted in salute. Then they began to climb the mountain trail once again.

Brian had been quiet during the whole long trip. Now he stopped so suddenly that Megan, who was following close behind, nearly ran into him.

"Megan," he said, "I want to thank you for . . . well, trusting me. I really needed that, more than anything else right now."

Glad that he could not see her in the darkness, Megan felt a rush of blood color her cheeks.

"Oh . . . come on," she said shortly. "If you don't soon get me up to the shed you're going to have to carry me. I'm so tired I could drop."

16

2:00 P.M., Sunday, September 17, 1889

September sun lay its golden blessing on the town. Megan could feel the lovely warmth of it deep in her bones, through the thin, fine lawn of her dress. She was wearing a pretty new hat, and from time to time she tilted its wide brim a bit to look up at Brian. They were walking side by side down the new board sidewalk that edged Birch Street.

Brian looked down at her with a grin.

"You really think you're something in that hat, don't you? And your hair all piled up high, like a regular lady!"

She flashed a smile at him. "Do you like it?"

"I guess," he admitted, "it's just about the prettiest *hat* I've ever seen."

"Oh, you!" She pretended to pout. "Well, anyway, Stefan thinks I'm pretty, don't you, Stefan?"

She gazed down at the small boy holding her hand. He gave her a sunny smile, his blue eyes sparkling.

"Here we are," Brian said, stopping before a new small frame house.

A pot of red geraniums shone on the steps. The old man who was sitting in a rocking chair on the porch waved to them.

"It's about time," he called. "I thought you would never come."

Megan let go of Brian's arm and quickly ran up the steps. She embraced the frail old figure.

"Oh, Mr. Shaw! I'm so glad to see you! You're looking marvelously well. Come, Stefan. . . ."

The little boy happily kissed the soft old cheek.

"Yes, well . . . now." Septimus Shaw beamed. "Let me look at all of you—such a fine-looking bunch. . . ."

Megan settled into the chair Brian had brought for her.

"It's wonderful to have you up and about again," she said, "and looking so fine."

"He's really not at all well," Brian had told her when he came to pick her up that day. "That pneumonia really laid him low. After all, he is eighty-seven, you know! When you think of what he's been through! But he pretends, and so you must pretend, too. He does so much want to see you."

Septimus Shaw smoothed the wool shawl that lay across his knees. Megan could see blue veins through the papery skin of his fine-boned hands.

"Mr. and Mrs. Alderson have been so good to us," he smiled, "having Brian and me here to live with them. And I am getting stronger every day."

He smiled with great fondness at Brian.

"Pretty soon this young giant won't have to be lifting me in and out of chairs—I'll be doing it for myself."

"You're darn right," Brian laughed. "But it's really building my muscles. Look!" And he flexed his arm.

Megan laughed. "Of course, hauling all that lumber and brick doesn't have a thing to do with it!"

Brian grinned enthusiastically. "Do you know, our crew put up two houses last week—two in one week!"

"At that rate," Septimus said proudly, "Johnstown will be rebuilt by Christmas."

Brian had been hired by one of the new construction companies.

"It pays good, too," he confided to Megan. "Mr. Shaw and I were figuring the other day, and we reckon that when the construction job ends, if I can get a job over at the Cambria Iron Works, why in about two years I'll have saved enough money to start college."

"Oh, Brian, that's wonderful," Megan cried.

Stefan had seated himself on the porch steps and was quietly playing with a ball and jacks he had taken from his pocket.

Septimus Shaw glanced at him and then back at Megan. A shadow crossed his face, and he shook his head slowly.

"Still no word?"

Megan looked at Stefan, who was busy with his jack game.

"No," she replied sadly. "Papa has had the finest doctors in the state. They all say the same thing—there's no physical reason why he can't talk. They're certain he can hear. They all say that when shock is deep enough, something happens in the mind. They just don't know if he'll ever speak again."

"Oh, what a pity," Septimus said. "And he seems so happy now. Brian tells me that no trace has ever been found of his family—if he is one of the Novaks. It was so good of your family to take him in and give him a home."

"Oh, but it's such a joy to us to have him," Megan replied. "When we found we'd lost Tim . . . well, it's been good for all of us to have Stefan."

She could think about it now, finally. The bodies of Timothy and Aunt Ella had been found five days after the flood, many miles downriver from Johnstown.

"Yes, well. . . ." Septimus cleared his throat. "Who knows? Maybe, in time. . . ."

His bleak old eyes took on a dreaming look.

"It is an amazing thing, the power of love. The power of caring. I really think that is what brought us through all of it—the fact that we cared about one another. . . ."

Megan glanced up. Brian was looking at her so earnestly that she felt her throat tighten. Color flooded her face.

"I—I wonder what ever happened to Daisy?" she said, flustered.

"Well, I do remember hearing that the *Night Off* company gave a benefit performance for the flood victims. So they must have got to Altoona all right."

"I wonder if Daisy ever found her trunk, with her red silk dress?"

"More's to the point," Brian said sourly, "I wonder if she ever found Tom?"

Megan gave a fleeting thought to Tom Hewitt scooping up the money and to Tom pulling Horace Fitch's watch from his pocket that morning in the shed. Much later she had learned that Horace Fitch had died in the first onrush of the flood waters, pinned beneath a rafter of his own house. He had never "given" Tom his beloved watch.

"I don't think Daisy would care," she said and shrugged. "I think Daisy was a lot smarter than the rest of us, or than me anyway."

In the manner of the very old, Septimus Shaw had dozed off to sleep in his chair. Megan straightened the shawl on his lap and kissed his forehead softly. They tiptoed down the steps of the porch.

"If I live to be a hundred," Megan said, as they walked

down the street together, "I will never forget that first morning, finding him standing on the porch shaving."

Brian laughed. "He's sure some old guy!"

"You know," she reflected, "that really taught me a lesson in self-respect."

Brian grinned at her.

"Well, in that hat you're really loaded with it!"

Megan began to laugh.

"I know what let's do," she said. "Let's borrow Papa's buggy and drive up to Green Hill. I'd like to see what the whole town looks like."

The afternoon shadows were lengthening, and the only Sabbath sounds were the steady clip-clop of the horse's feet on the dusty road and the long downhill slide of cicada song from the goldenrod in the ditches.

The three in the buggy were silent, content just to be together. Brian drew the horse to a halt at a place where the road curved back on itself. Johnstown lay before them like a town in a picture book.

He helped Megan and lifted Stefan down. They stood together, looking at the scene.

Nearly four months had elapsed since the terrible wave had engulfed Johnstown. Finally, when it was all over, there were over two thousand dead and countless numbers homeless. There was a new cemetery at Grandview, filled with row upon row of unnamed crosses.

The whole world, reeling with shock at the horror of the disaster, had rallied to help. Money and supplies came from as far away as the Lord Mayor of Dublin and the Sultan of Turkey, as well as from towns and cities all across the United States.

The people of Johnstown had begun to rebuild their city.

Maxwell and Foster had a new store on Main Street, and the hotel and banks had been rebuilt. There was a new Catholic church going up, and the Cambria Iron Works had begun production.

You could see streets now where none had been before. There were still great piles of wreckage—lumber and railroad cars and wire fence lying about—but in between new houses were going up. Some were still frame skeletons of beams, but others, completed, glistened with fresh paint in the westering sun.

Patches of green showed where new lawns were starting, and here and there were brave bursts of color from flower gardens. From over across town a puff of white smoke drifted from a train, and the low, sweet call of its whistle could be heard.

The bell on the Lutheran church boomed five.

"Look, Brian," Megan said, "over there, where the hospital tents were. They're putting up houses."

Brian reached down and took her hand.

"You know, Megs, I was really proud of you—the way you worked."

She looked up at him, her eyes flashing.

"Well, who wouldn't work for Miss Barton? She was . . . oh, Brian, she was really . . . magnificent!"

The Johnstown Flood had been the first time that the newly formed Red Cross had been given an opportunity to show how it could be of help in a disaster. Miss Clara Barton had arrived a week after the flood with medical supplies and a few trained nurses. She had immediately set up hospital tents and had supervised the only organized medical care in the stricken valley. Many of the townswomen had volunteered as nurses, and Megan had been one of the most faithful.

"You know," Megan continued slowly, "I've been doing a lot of thinking. I haven't mentioned this to anyone, not even Papa and Mama. But, Brian . . . well, I guess I wanted to talk to you first."

She hesitated and then went on speaking.

"Do you think, just maybe . . . that I might be able to train as a . . . nurse?"

Brian looked at her animated face beneath the pretty wide-brimmed hat. Then he squeezed her hand hard.

"Why sure! Why not? I think it's a great idea! After all, anyone who can ride out the Johnstown Flood on a mattress can do *anything*!"

About the Author

Marden Dahlstedt was born and grew up in Pittsburgh, Pennsylvania, and was graduated from Chatham College. About *The Terrible Wave* she writes: "My interest in the Johnstown Flood stems from the fact that my grandparents survived it. They were newly married at the time, and my grandfather was an engineer on the Pennsylvania Railroad. He had taken his train to Altoona that morning, and around noon that day a friend, who had a farm in the mountains, came into town and took my grandmother home with him in a wagon. It was nearly a week before either knew the other was safe. So I grew up with family stories of the flood, some of which have been incorporated in *The Terrible Wave*."

Mrs. Dahlstedt lives with her husband, Richard Dahlstedt, in Beach Haven Gardens, New Jersey, where she owns and operates an antique shop during the summer and writes a weekly newspaper column on antiques.

About the Artist

Charles Robinson is a graduate of Milton Academy, Harvard College, and the University of Virginia Law School. A member of the New Jersey bar, he gave up practicing law in 1968 to devote full time to the illustration of children's books and has been remarkably successful. He wrote and illustrated *Yuri and the Mooneygoats* and has illustrated more than forty other books for young readers, including *Journey to America, The Mother Tree, Chibia the Dhow Boy,* and *The Pup with the Up-and-Down Tail.*

Charles Robinson, his wife, Cynthia, and their three children live in New Vernon, New Jersey.